BUSINESS ISSUES, COMPETITION AND ENTREPRENEURSHIP

BUSINESS TAXATION

ORGANIZATIONAL CHOICES AND FEDERAL CONSIDERATIONS

Business Issues, Competition and Entrepreneurship

Additional books in this series can be found on Nova's website under the Series tab.

Additional E-books in this series can be found on Nova's website under the E-book tab.

Economic Issues, Problems and Perspectives

Additional books in this series can be found on Nova's website under the Series tab.

Additional E-books in this series can be found on Nova's website under the E-book tab.

BUSINESS ISSUES, COMPETITION AND ENTREPRENEURSHIP

BUSINESS TAXATION

ORGANIZATIONAL CHOICES AND FEDERAL CONSIDERATIONS

JAMES C. TEAGUE
AND
KARLY FAWNER
EDITORS

NOVINKA

New York

For permission to use material from this book please contact us:
Telephone 631-231-7269; Fax 631-231-8175
Web Site: http://www.novapublishers.com

Additional color graphics may be available in the e-book version of this book.

LIBRARY OF CONGRESS CATALOGING-IN-PUBLICATION DATA

ISBN: 978-1-62257-998-3

Published by Nova Science Publishers, Inc. † New York

CONTENTS

PREFACE

In the United States, how a business is taxed at the federal level is partly dependent on how it is organized. Publicly traded corporations known as subchapter C corporations are taxed once at the corporate level according to the corporate tax system, and then a second time at the individual-shareholder level according to the individual tax system when corporate dividend payments are made or capital gains are realized. This leads to the so-called "double taxation" of corporate profits. Businesses that choose any other form of organization are, in general, taxed only once at the individual level. That is, the income of certain businesses passes through to the individual business owners and is taxed according to the individual income tax system. Examples of these alternative "pass-through" forms of organization include sole proprietorships, partnerships, subchapter S corporations, and limited liability companies. This book summarizes the general tax treatment of corporate and pass-through businesses and analyzes the most recent business data from the Internal Revenue Service (IRS).

Chapter 1 – In the United States, how a business is taxed at the federal level is partly dependent on how it is organized. Publicly traded corporations known as subchapter C corporations are taxed once at the corporate level according to the corporate tax system, and then a second time at the individual-shareholder level according to the individual tax system when corporate dividend payments are made or capital gains are realized. This leads to the so-called "double taxation" of corporate profits. Businesses that choose any other form of organization are, in general, taxed only once at the individual level. That is, the income of certain businesses passes through to the individual business owners and is taxed according to the individual income tax system. Examples of these alternative "pass-through" forms of organization include sole proprietorships, partnerships, subchapter S corporations, and limited liability companies.

This report summarizes the general tax treatment of corporate and pass-through businesses and analyzes the most recent business data from the Internal Revenue Service (IRS). Analysis of the data shows that the majority of businesses in this country are small. The analysis also reveals that most businesses are of the pass-through variety, which raises the likelihood that a large fraction of businesses are taxed according to the individual tax system, not the corporate tax system. Businesses that do pay the corporate income tax (i.e., C corporations) are, however, much larger and account for the majority of business activity, which indicates that their share of business taxes paid is likely higher than non-corporate entities. Extending the analysis back to 1980 makes it clear that the pass-through forms of organization have increased in popularity over time at the expense of the corporate form.

Understanding how businesses are taxed provides context for understanding current and future proposals to adjust either the individual or corporate income tax rates. Currently, both the top individual and the top corporate tax rates are 35%. However, President Obama's FY2011 budget proposes allowing the top individual tax rate to revert to its pre-2001 level of 39.6%. Future proposals in Congress could be similar to the Administration's proposal, or, if past proposals are any indication, move in the opposite direction. For example, in the 110th Congress then-Chairman of the House Ways and Means Committee Charles Rangel introduced a proposal (H.R. 3970) that would have lowered the top corporate tax rate from 35% to 30.5%.

In response to either an increase in the top individual tax rates or a decrease in the top corporate tax rate, economic theory and data would suggest that some pass-through businesses could choose to reorganize as C corporations to take advantage of the more favorable corporate tax schedule. In addition, although the President's budget proposal would raise individual tax rates, it could have the effect of raising taxes on some businesses because data presented in this report indicate that most businesses are likely taxed according to the individual income tax schedule, and may be at the top bracket.

More recently, S. 2343, the Stop the Student Loan Interest Rate Hike of 2012, would reduce the interest rate from 6.8% to 3.4% on Subsidized Stafford Loans made to undergraduate students during academic year 2012 - 2013. To offset the increase in mandatory spending, the bill would require taxpayers with modified adjusted gross income in excess of $250,000 to pay self-employment taxes (Social Security and Medicare) on certain income currently exempt from self-employment taxes if that income is received from a professional service partnership or a professional service S corporation in which at least 75% of gross income is attributable to three or fewer shareholders. The offset is estimated to raise $9.0 billion from FY2012 to FY2022.

Chapter 2 – A foundation of the broad tax revisions implemented 24 years ago by the Tax Reform Act of 1986 was tax "neutrality"—the idea that economic efficiency and economic welfare are promoted if the distorting impact of taxes on business and other economic decisions is minimized. Based on this principle, the 1986 act broadened the tax base and reduced statutory tax rates set forth by the tax code. In time, however, the underlying thrust of tax policy has changed. Rather than neutrality and efficiency, recent business tax legislation has been guided more by a concern for promoting investment and capital formation, and by attention to the perceived impact of taxes on the ability of U.S. firms to compete with foreign companies. Further, recent interest in fundamental tax reform has been partly stimulated by these same concerns for capital formation and competitiveness.

Twenty-four years after the 1986 act, business tax policy is thus potentially at a crossroads, and it is useful to take stock of where the system stands, the economic effects it is known to have, and the principal options for reform. Several data series show a similar pattern in the level of corporate taxes: corporate income taxes have generally declined over the post-World War II period. At the same time, however, significant disparities in the structure of business taxes have remained, suggesting a persistence of distortions caused by the tax system: corporate-sector investment remains heavily taxed compared to non-corporate business and owner-occupied housing; debt is favored over equity; and equipment is favored over structures.

The base of business taxation is the return to business investment; business taxes thus influence the economy through their impact on investment. In broad terms, business taxes can, at least in principle, reduce capital formation and thus impair long-term economic growth by making saving and investment less attractive. This effect, however, depends on a robust saving response to taxes, the presence of which is uncertain. Another impact is on the allocation of investment among different sectors and asset types. Here, business taxes likely distort investment decisions, reducing economic efficiency and economic welfare. In the case of equity, economic theory suggests that in the long run, the burden of business taxation is shared among all owners of capital and has a progressive effect on the tax system.

Various hypothetical alternatives exist for reforming the business tax system. One possibility is to move in the direction of the 1986 Tax Reform Act by broadening the existing tax base—that is, by eliminating tax benefits and preferences. Another possibility—and one that is favored by many economists—is to adopt some form of tax integration that would eliminate the double taxation of corporate income. A third option is to adopt a form of consumption tax, under which new business investment would be exempt from tax. Either corporate tax integration or a consumption tax could improve economic efficiency, but only if the design were to avoid the types of distortions present in the current system.

Chapter 3 – Several lawmakers and the Obama Administration have expressed interest in taxing large partnerships and S corporations, also known as pass-throughs, as corporations. Part of this interest appears to be related to deficit and debt concerns. Pass-throughs may be a source of revenue since they currently account for over half of all business income but generally pay no corporate tax. Additionally, there is a growing concern that the current business tax environment may be inequitable and inefficient. Today, two business that are otherwise identical except that one is a corporation and the other is a pass-through are taxed differently. This disparity could be viewed as inequitable since the companies are similarly positioned to pay taxes.

Additionally, the lack of tax uniformity across business types may cause an inefficient allocation of resources if business decisions are made for tax reasons and not economic reasons. This report uses aggregate and industry-level tax data to analyze how many partnerships and S corporations could be subject to the corporate tax. It is estimated that if a receipt-based measure of size is used, then between 0.3% and 1.5% of S corporations and partnerships could be taxed as corporations depending on if a "large" pass-through is defined as one with receipts exceeding \$50 million or exceeding \$10 million. Using an asset-based measure of size produces similar estimates. It is estimated that between 0.3% and 1.0% of pass-throughs could pay the corporate tax depending on whether a \$100 million or \$25 million asset threshold is used to define a "large" firm.

Although estimates suggest that only a small percentage of pass-throughs could be considered large for corporate tax purposes, this report also finds that those firms are responsible for a significant amount of economic activity, indicating that the proposed policy change could raise substantial revenue. For example, 30% of S corporation receipts are generated by the largest 0.3% of S corporations, and 41% of partnership receipts are generated by the largest 0.2% of partnerships. Similarly, the largest 0.2% of S corporations hold 43%

of S corporation assets, while the largest 1.1% of partnerships hold 78% of partnership assets.

Taxing large pass-throughs as corporations would also allow for lower tax rates as it would broaden the corporate tax base. Lower tax rates combined with a reduction in the tax disparity between the corporate and non-corporate sectors could improve business tax equity and the allocation of resources relative to current policy. At the same time, an alternative policy prescription that is generally more appealing to economists—integration of the corporate and individual tax systems—could also achieve these objectives. If integration is not possible, however, then reducing the tax discrepancy between large pass-throughs and corporations may be another viable alternative, depending on its design.

Chapter 4 – Pass-through businesses – sole proprietorships, partnerships, and S corporations – generate more than half of all business income in the United States. Pass-through income is, in general, taxed only once at the individual income tax rates when it is distributed to its owners. In contrast, the income of C corporations is taxed twice; once at the corporate level according to corporate tax rates, and then a second time at the individual tax rates when shareholders receive dividend payments or realize capital gains. This leads to the so-called ""double taxation"" of corporate profits.

This report analyzes individual tax return data to determine who earns pass-through business income and bears the burden of taxes on that income. The analysis finds that over 82% of net pass-through income is earned by taxpayers with an adjusted gross income (AGI) over $100,000, although these taxpayers account for just 23% of returns filed. A significant fraction of pass-through income is concentrated among upper-income earners. Taxpayers with AGI over $250,000, for example, receive 62% of pass-through income, but account for just over 6% of returns with pass-through income. A closer look at S corporations and partnerships shows passive income accounts for 10% and 25%, respectively, of their total income. This analysis, when combined with research on the corporate tax burden, suggests that higher-income taxpayers will generally bear most of the burden from increased pass-through taxes.

A number of proposed and scheduled tax changes would result in pass-throughs paying higher taxes. Several lawmakers and the Obama Administration, for example, have expressed interest in taxing large pass-throughs as corporations, which would subject some pass-throughs to an additional layer of taxation. Pass-through taxation could also increase if a tax reform that includes lower corporate tax rates that are paid for by the elimination or reduction of certain business tax benefits is enacted.

Additionally, the scheduled expiration of the 2001/2003 tax cuts at the end of this year could increase taxes on pass-throughs by increasing individual tax rates. Lastly, a new 3.8% tax on passive income that was enacted as part of the Health Care and Education Reconciliation Act of 2010 (HCERA, P.L. 111-152) is set to take effect in 2013. The tax may apply to some pass-throughs.

While the analysis of these proposed and scheduled changes suggests that higher-income taxpayers will generally bear most of the burden from increased pass-through taxes, there are circumstances that could raise congressional concern. For example, an across-the-board expiration of the 2001/2003 individual tax rates will increase taxes for all pass-through owners. One option for preventing the tax burden from increasing for lower and middle class business owners is to allow the reduced rates to expire only for higher-income earners.

Concern has also risen over the new 3.8% tax on passive income and its effect on pass-throughs. The distributional analysis in this report shows, however, most S corporation and partnership income is the active type, and active business income is exempt from the 3.8% tax. The share of income that is passive, and potentially subject to the new tax, overwhelmingly accrues to higher-income taxpayers——77% of passive partnership income and 93% of passive S corporation income went to taxpayers with AGI over $250,000. Sole proprietors could generally be expected to be exempt from the tax since most of their income is likely active.

Chapter 5 – Corporate tax revenues have declined over the last six decades. In the post-World War II era, corporate tax revenue as a percentage of gross domestic product (GDP) peaked in 1952 at 6.1%. Today, the corporate tax generates revenue equal to approximately 1.3% of GDP. The corporate tax has also decreased in importance relative to other revenue sources. At its post-WWII peak in 1952, the corporate tax generated 32.1% of all federal tax revenue. In that same year the individual tax accounted for 42.2% of federal revenue, and the payroll tax accounted for 9.7% of revenue. Today, the corporate tax accounts for 8.9% of federal tax revenue, whereas the individual and payroll taxes generate 41.5% and 40.0%, respectively, of federal revenue.

This report discusses the three main factors for the decline in corporate tax revenue. First, the average effective corporate tax rate has decreased over time, mostly as a result of reductions in the statutory rate and changes affecting the tax treatment of investment and capital recovery (depreciation). Second, an increasing fraction of business activity is being carried out by partnerships and S corporations, which are not subject to the corporate income tax. This has led to an erosion of the corporate tax base. And third, corporate sector profitability has fallen over time, leading to a further erosion of the corporate tax base.

Understanding the decline in corporate tax revenue could be helpful in preserving any tax reforms enacted, or structuring a reform to obtain a desired revenue effect, such as revenue neutrality or enhancement. The House Committee on Ways and Means and the Senate Committee on Finance have held hearings on tax reform throughout the first session of the 112th Congress. The President, in his 2011 State of the Union address, called for corporate tax reform that did not add to the deficit. Generally, the corporate reform discussion has focused on reducing statutory rates and achieving revenue neutrality through broadening the tax base by eliminating various deductions, exemptions, and credits, among other things.

Corporate tax revenues have been declining for the last six decades. This report discusses the three main factors for the decline. First, the average effective corporate tax rate has decreased over time, mostly due to reductions in the statutory rate and changes affecting the tax treatment of investment and capital recovery (depreciation). Second, an increasing fraction of business activity is being carried out by partnerships and S corporations, which are not subject to the corporate income tax. This has led to an erosion of the corporate tax base. And third, corporate sector profitability has fallen over time, leading to a further erosion of the corporate tax base.

As Congress considers options for tax reform, background on the decline in corporate tax revenue could prove useful in preserving any tax reforms enacted, or structuring a reform to obtain a desired revenue effect, such as revenue neutrality or enhancement. The House Committee on Ways and Means and the Senate Committee on Finance have held hearings on tax reform throughout the first session of the 112th Congress. In his 2011 State of the Union address the President called for corporate tax reform that did not add to the deficit. Generally, the corporate reform discussion has focused on reducing statutory rates and achieving revenue neutrality through broadening the tax base by eliminating various deductions, exemptions, and credits, among other things, such as shifting to a territorial tax system.

This report begins by documenting the decline in corporate tax revenue. An analysis of the three main factors explaining this decline is then presented. The data and calculations used in this report may be found in Appendix. The analysis in this report focuses only on nonfinancial corporations for two reasons. First, nonfinancial corporations are the firms primarily affected by investment- and depreciation-related tax changes since they account for the majority of physical capital investment. Second, the bulk of revenue that is generated from the corporate tax comes from taxing nonfinancial companies.

In: Business Taxation
Editors: J. C. Teague and K. Fawner
ISBN: 978-1-62257-998-3

Chapter 1

BUSINESS ORGANIZATIONAL CHOICES: TAXATION AND RESPONSES TO LEGISLATIVE CHANGES*

Mark P. Keightley

SUMMARY

In the United States, how a business is taxed at the federal level is partly dependent on how it is organized. Publicly traded corporations known as subchapter C corporations are taxed once at the corporate level according to the corporate tax system, and then a second time at the individual-shareholder level according to the individual tax system when corporate dividend payments are made or capital gains are realized. This leads to the so-called "double taxation" of corporate profits. Businesses that choose any other form of organization are, in general, taxed only once at the individual level. That is, the income of certain businesses passes through to the individual business owners and is taxed according to the individual income tax system. Examples of these alternative "pass-through" forms of organization include sole proprietorships, partnerships, subchapter S corporations, and limited liability companies.

This report summarizes the general tax treatment of corporate and pass-through businesses and analyzes the most recent business data from

---

* This is an edited, reformatted and augmented version of a Congressional Research Service publication, CRS Report for Congress R40748, from www.crs.gov, prepared for Members and Committees of Congress, dated April 26, 2012.

the Internal Revenue Service (IRS). Analysis of the data shows that the majority of businesses in this country are small. The analysis also reveals that most businesses are of the pass-through variety, which raises the likelihood that a large fraction of businesses are taxed according to the individual tax system, not the corporate tax system. Businesses that do pay the corporate income tax (i.e., C corporations) are, however, much larger and account for the majority of business activity, which indicates that their share of business taxes paid is likely higher than non-corporate entities. Extending the analysis back to 1980 makes it clear that the pass-through forms of organization have increased in popularity over time at the expense of the corporate form.

Understanding how businesses are taxed provides context for understanding current and future proposals to adjust either the individual or corporate income tax rates. Currently, both the top individual and the top corporate tax rates are 35%. However, President Obama's FY2011 budget proposes allowing the top individual tax rate to revert to its pre-2001 level of 39.6%. Future proposals in Congress could be similar to the Administration's proposal, or, if past proposals are any indication, move in the opposite direction. For example, in the 110th Congress then-Chairman of the House Ways and Means Committee Charles Rangel introduced a proposal (H.R. 3970) that would have lowered the top corporate tax rate from 35% to 30.5%.

In response to either an increase in the top individual tax rates or a decrease in the top corporate tax rate, economic theory and data would suggest that some pass-through businesses could choose to reorganize as C corporations to take advantage of the more favorable corporate tax schedule. In addition, although the President's budget proposal would raise individual tax rates, it could have the effect of raising taxes on some businesses because data presented in this report indicate that most businesses are likely taxed according to the individual income tax schedule, and may be at the top bracket.

More recently, S. 2343, the Stop the Student Loan Interest Rate Hike of 2012, would reduce the interest rate from 6.8% to 3.4% on Subsidized Stafford Loans made to undergraduate students during academic year 2012 - 2013. To offset the increase in mandatory spending, the bill would require taxpayers with modified adjusted gross income in excess of $250,000 to pay self-employment taxes (Social Security and Medicare) on certain income currently exempt from self-employment taxes if that income is received from a professional service partnership or a professional service S corporation in which at least 75% of gross income is attributable to three or fewer shareholders. The offset is estimated to raise $9.0 billion from FY2012 to FY2022.

INTRODUCTION

In the United States, how a business is taxed at the federal level is partly dependent on how it is organized. Publicly traded corporations known as subchapter C corporations are taxed once at the corporate level according to the corporate tax system, and then a second time at the individual-shareholder level according to the individual tax system when corporate dividend payments are made or capital gains are realized. This leads to the so-called "double taxation" of corporate profits. Businesses that choose any other form of organization are, in general, taxed only once at the individual level. That is, the income of certain businesses passes through to the individual business owners and is taxed according to the individual income tax system. Examples of these alternative "pass-through" forms of organization include sole proprietorships, partnerships, subchapter S corporations, and limited liability companies.[1]

Economic theory and historical data suggest that businesses may respond to tax policy changes by reorganizing to reduce their tax liability. For example, an analysis of the most recent Internal Revenue Service (IRS) data indicates that such a response seems to have occurred following the Tax Reform Act of 1986 (TRA86; P.L. 99-514). Among other things, TRA86 lowered the top individual tax rate below the top corporate tax rate. This appears to have provided an incentive for some C corporations to reorganize as pass-throughs to take advantage of the lower individual rates. In line with this reasoning, the fraction of businesses organized as C corporations had fallen from 14.9% to 10.3% (or 31%) within five years of the rate changes.

While both the top individual and the top corporate tax rates are currently 35%, there have been recent proposals made by the Administration and in Congress to change these rates. President Obama's proposed FY2011 budget would allow the top individual tax rate to revert to its pre-2001 level of 39.6% while leaving the top corporate rate at 35%. In the 110th Congress, then-Chairman of the House Ways and Means Committee Charles Rangel introduced H.R. 3970, the Tax Reduction and Reform Act, which would have lowered the top corporate tax rate from 35% to 30.5%. Future proposals could use H.R. 3970 as a template. In response to either one of these proposals, past behavior and economic theory would indicate that the number of C corporations as a fraction of total businesses could increase.

More recently, S. 2343, the Stop the Student Loan Interest Rate Hike of 2012, would reduce the interest rate from 6.8% to 3.4% on Subsidized Stafford Loans made to undergraduate students during academic year 2012-2013. To offset the increase in mandatory spending, it would require taxpayers with modified adjusted gross income in excess of $250,000 to pay self-employment taxes (Social Security and Medicare) on certain income currently exempt from self-employment taxes if that income is received from a professional service partnership or a professional service S corporation in which at least 75% of gross income is attributable to three or fewer shareholders. The offset is estimated to raise $9.0 billion from FY2012 to FY2022.[2]

This report provides a general overview of the tax treatment of the major forms of business organization. Included in the overview presented in the body of the report is a discussion of sole proprietorships, partnerships, C corporations, subchapter S corporations, and limited liability companies. Other less popular, but still important, forms of business organization are discussed in the *Appendix*.

This report also analyzes the most recent data from the IRS on business organization. The analysis shows that the majority of businesses in this country are and historically have been of the pass-through variety.

That is, most businesses in the United States are likely to be taxed according to the individual tax system, not the corporate tax system. Businesses that do pay the corporate income tax (i.e., C corporations) are, however, much larger and account for the majority of business activity, which indicates that their share of business taxes paid is likely high. The analysis also shows that the distribution of businesses has changed over time, in what many economists view as a response to certain legislative changes that affected businesses.

A number of important issues relating to business taxation are beyond the scope of this paper.

Forms of Business Organization

The five major forms of business organization are sole proprietorships, partnerships, C corporations, S corporations, and limited liability companies.[3] While a number of factors come into play when choosing how to organize, two of the most important are how the business will be treated for tax purposes and legal purposes.

The laws covering the various forms of organization evolved separately and have never been fully integrated. The following section provides a general overview of the differences that exist among the most popular organizational forms.

Sole Proprietorships

A sole proprietorship is an unincorporated, single-owner business that is treated as identical with its owner. That is, a sole proprietorship is "disregarded" as separate from its owner for federal tax purposes. The sole proprietorship is the most common and basic form of business organization. Unlike some other forms of business organization, a sole proprietorship does not provide its owner with limited liability. The business assets of the proprietorship as well as the personal assets of its owner may be used to settle any legal judgment against the business. In contrast, limited liability provides some protection for the personal assets of an owner from judgments against the business.

The business income of a sole proprietorship is reported on the owner's individual income tax return and taxed at the applicable individual income tax rates. Taxable business income includes net profits distributed to the owner as well as retained earnings. In addition, a sole proprietor is responsible for paying the self-employment tax. The self-employment tax rate is 15.3% and is composed of two parts: a Medicare tax (2.9%) and a social security tax (12.4%). In 2009, only the first $106,800 of self-employment income is subject to the social security portion of the tax. The tax is analogous to the combined employer's and employee's share of the Social Security and Medicare taxes, half of which is a payroll tax withheld by most employers.

Partnerships

A partnership is a joint venture consisting of at least two partners organized to operate a trade or business with each partner sharing profits, losses, deductions, credits, and the like.[4] A partner is an investor in such an entity and may be an individual, a trust, a partnership, a corporation, another entity (such as a limited liability company), or a broker that is holding the ownership interest of an unnamed partner. Partnerships are established under the individual laws of each state, although their tax treatment at the federal level is determined by the Internal Revenue Code (IRC). The most common partnerships, which are discussed below, include general partnerships, limited liability partnerships, limited partnerships, publicly traded partnerships, and electing large partnerships.

One of the most important components of a partnership is the partnership agreement.[5] The partnership agreement is a comprehensive agreement among the partners that specifies such things as the partnership's name and purpose, partner contributions, management responsibilities, and continuity of the partnership should a partner leave.[6] Most importantly, the partnership agreement specifies in what ratio business income, losses, deductions, and credits are passed-through the partnership and split among the partners. It is common for these items to be divided according to the ownership interests of the partners, although there is no requirement that this be the case.

Tax Treatment of Partnerships

Partnerships themselves are not taxable; instead all tax items such as income, losses, deductions, and credits, pass through the partnership to the partners. The partnership reports each partner's allocation to the IRS and to the partners according to the partnership agreement. The partners then include their share of income or loss on their own tax return, even if there was no actual distribution of income to the partners. As long as there are no corporate partners, taxable business income is taxed only once according to the individual income tax schedule. When a partnership does have a corporate partner, the share of income allocated to that partner may eventually be taxed at corporate rates.

Although the partnership agreement determines the final allocation of tax items to each partner, the partnership must distinguish between ordinary income and separately stated items when making the allocation. Some items must be stated separately because the partners may face limitations to the degree to which they may utilize certain tax items. For example, a capital loss may affect partners differently if some are able to use it to offset a capital gain. Separately stated items include capital gains and losses, dividends, tax-exempt interest, rents, royalties, deductions attributable to portfolio income, charitable contributions, foreign taxes paid, and special allocation items determined by the partnership agreement. Ordinary income is the sum of income, gains, losses, and deductions that need not be separately stated.[7]

In addition to being entitled to a share of the partnership's profits or losses, partners may also be given guaranteed payments for their contributions of capital or service. Such payments are fixed and do not depend on the profitability of the firm. Fringe benefits such as health insurance are also considered a guaranteed payment. The partnership deducts guaranteed payments as ordinary business expenses, and the partners include them as ordinary income. To the extent that the guaranteed payments are for personal services performed by a partner, the income would be subject to self-employment tax.

General Partnerships

A general partnership is one in which all partners are liable for the actions and debts of the business.[8] That is, the business assets of the partnership, as well as the assets of the partners, may be used to settle a legal judgment against the business. Each partner is also responsible for the management of the company and for the tax reporting required of the partnership to the IRS.[9] If there is disagreement among the partners, the IRS considers them all responsible. The defining features of a general partnership make it useful to consider it a direct extension of a sole proprietorship to multiple individuals.

Limited Liability Partnerships

A limited liability partnership (LLP) is a general partnership, usually a professional firm, in which the partners are mutually liable for the partnership debts but are protected from the harmful actions of the other partners. Each partner is liable only for damages arising from his or her own harmful actions and those of their subordinates. However, there are differences regarding liability that vary from state to state. In all other ways, an LLP is like a general partnership.

LLPs are a recent creation of state law, but they have become especially popular with legal and accounting firms. The organizational form of choice for large accounting firms is currently the LLP.[10]

Limited Partnerships

A limited partnership consists of at least one general partner and one or more limited partners. The general partners oversee the management of the business and are liable for the partnership's debts. The liability of the other partners is limited to their capital contribution and any additional amounts specified in the partnership agreement. Limited partners cannot take part in the management of the partnership. The general partners are responsible for the all partnership filings required by the IRS. The partnership's income and losses are allocated among the general and limited partners according to the partnership agreement. Partners are each responsible for any income tax on their share of the partnership income. However, limited partners who do not perform a service for the partnership are not considered self-employed and therefore are not responsible for self-employment tax unless they receive guaranteed payments for services performed for the partnership.

Limited partnerships are often used as investment vehicles, for example, in oil and gas exploration. In such a case, the actual drilling parent company serves as the general partner, and the investors owning shares of the venture are treated as limited partners.

Publicly Traded Partnership

A publicly traded partnership (PTP) is one whose ownership interests are traded on an established exchange or in a secondary market or its equivalent. In general, a PTP is treated as a C corporation (discussed below) for tax purposes, and therefore subject to the corporate income tax. There are, however, two exceptions to this general rule. The first exception affects partnerships with at least 90% of their gross income from passive investments, such as dividends, interest, rents, capital gains, and mining and natural resource income.[11] A passive loss generated by a publicly traded partnership may not be used to offset income from other investments, only passive income from the corresponding PTP. The second exception affects partnerships that were publicly traded on December 17, 1987. These partnerships may elect to retain partnership status by paying a tax equal to 3.5% of gross income from the active conduct of business as long as the line of business is unaltered.[12]

Electing Large Partnerships

Under certain circumstances a partnership may elect to be treated as a large partnership with simplified tax reporting requirements. Generally, a non-service partnership with at least 100 partners may elect large partnership status. The category "electing large partnerships" was created by the Taxpayer Relief Act of 1997 (P.L. 105-34) to simplify the reporting requirements for investors in large partnerships.

Electing to be treated as a large partnership simplifies reporting by reducing the number of tax items that must be reported separately at the partnership level. A separate allocation is required only for tax-exempt interest, passive loss limitation and alternative minimum tax items, foreign taxes, and some tax credits.[13] Everything else is netted at the partnership level, and net income or loss is allocated to the partners.14 Most tax audits and tax adjustments take place at the partnership level, with partners notified of their share of any changes.

C Corporations

An alternative to the sole proprietorship or partnership forms of organization is the corporate form. Two types of corporate forms exist: C corporations, which are discussed in this section, and S corporations, which are discussed in the following section. C corporations, also known as ordinary corporations, are named for Subchapter C of the IRC, which details their tax treatment. Businesses incorporate under state law, and the exact requirements for incorporation may vary from state to state. Generally, in order to incorporate, a business must first file articles of incorporation at the state level.[15] The articles of incorporation generally state the name of the corporation, describe the general business or trade that will be conducted, authorize the number and type of shares to be issued, and define the powers of the board of directors.

For legal purposes, a C corporation is an entity that is separate from its owners (shareholders). As a result, shareholders are generally not liable for the actions of the corporation. Shareholders elect a board of directors, which in turn appoints and oversees the corporation's officers (e.g., CEO, COO, and CFO), who are responsible for the day-to-day management of the business. Shareholders can influence the operation of a corporation directly through their right to vote on certain matters, including the removal of elected corporate officials.

The corporate form of organization allows a business to take advantage of a number of benefits not available with other forms of organization. A C corporation, unlike an S corporation, faces no limits with respect to the number of shareholders it may have, the classes of stocks it may issue, or citizenship of its shareholders. Shares of C corporation stock are also traded on well developed exchanges, which allows ownership interests to be transferred readily and at low transaction costs. As a result, C corporations have the ability to raise capital globally from a variety of investors.

Tax Treatment of C Corporations

For tax purposes, the distinguishing feature of a C corporation is that it is a taxable entity. Income and other tax items (deductions, credits, etc.) do not flow directly through the corporation to its owners, as is the case with a sole proprietorship or partnership. Instead, business income is subject to taxation at the corporate level according to the corporate income tax schedule. Any after-tax income that is then distributed to shareholders in the form of dividends is taxed again according to the personal income tax schedule. This extra layer of taxation gives rise to what is known as the "double taxation" of corporate profits.

Because a corporation itself is a taxable entity and directly responsible for paying taxes, taxable income is computed at the corporate level. A corporation begins by aggregating all sources of business income to arrive at total income. Income sources include sales revenue, investment income, royalties, rents, and capital gains. To arrive at taxable income, the corporation then deducts business expenses and other special deductions. Deductions include such things as salaries and wages, bad debts, depreciation, advertising costs, and a portion of domestic production activities, among others. Corporations are also allowed to deduct interest paid to bond holders although not dividend payments made to shareholders. As a result, corporations may rely more on debt financing than they otherwise would.

Like individuals, a corporation may be required to compute its income tax liability twice, once according to the regular corporate tax, and again according to the corporate alternative minimum tax (AMT). A corporation must pay the higher of the two taxes. The AMT is designed to guarantee that corporations are subject to a minimum rate of taxation by limiting the degree to which they can utilize tax deductions and credits.

S Corporations

An S corporation is a closely held corporation that elects to be treated as a pass-through entity for tax purposes. S corporations are named for Subchapter S of the IRC, which details their tax treatment. By electing S corporation status, a business is able to combine many of the legal and business advantages of a C corporation with the tax advantages of a partnership.

Several criteria must be met if a corporation wishes to elect S corporation status. The corporation must be incorporated and organized in the United States. An S corporation can only issue one class of stock and is limited to no more than 100 shareholders.[16] The shareholders must be individuals, estates, certain types of trusts, tax-exempt pension funds, or charitable organizations. All shareholders must be U.S. citizens or residents. Certain banks, insurance companies, possession corporations, and other select business operations are ineligible to elect S corporate status.

An eligible corporation that seeks S corporation status must file a timely election with the IRS. Each shareholder must consent in writing to the election. The shareholders agree to report and pay tax on their shares of the corporation's income. The election can be revoked with the consent of shareholders holding more than 50% of the outstanding shares of stock. If an S corporation election is revoked, the corporation cannot elect S status for five years without the consent of the IRS.

Tax Treatment of S Corporations

S corporations generally do not pay income taxes. As with partnerships, operating income and loss are computed at the corporate level and passed through to the shareholders, while other items with special tax attributes are passed through separately. Separately stated items include portfolio income, capital gains and losses, passive income and losses, charitable contributions, foreign taxes paid, and the like. These tax items retain their character in the hands of the shareholders, who report allocations on their own returns, where the income is taxed for individuals. If the shareholder is a pass-through entity, the income is passed through the shareholder to the income beneficiaries of the pass-through entity.

An S corporation is not afforded the same flexibility as a partnership with respect to allocations amongst its owners. Because an S corporation is only permitted to issue one class of stock, all allocations must be proportionate to ownership. S corporation shareholders are not subject to self-employment taxes on items passed through the corporation. Like partners, shareholders who are also employees of the corporation may receive guaranteed salaries and fringe benefits. The corporation may deduct these expenses but must also pay employment taxes and withhold income and payroll taxes.

An area of contention between S corporations and the IRS is the structure of employee-shareholder compensation. Compensation in the form of regular wages or salary is generally subject to payroll taxes and unemployment taxes. Dividend compensation, however, avoids these taxes. This provides an incentive for S corporations to pay and employee-shareholders to receive dividends in lieu of wages or salary. The IRS has attempted to address this issue by reminding S corporations that they must pay "reasonable compensation" (subject to employment taxes) to shareholder-employees in return for services, before dividend compensation.[17] Compensation is considered reasonable when it matchers what the market return would be to the services provided by the employee. Failure to follow the IRS's suggestion could result in the reclassification of dividend compensation as wage or salary compensation for tax purposes.

More recently, S. 2343, the Stop the Student Loan Interest Rate Hike of 2012, would reduce the interest rate from 6.8% to 3.4% on Subsidized Stafford Loans made to undergraduate students during academic year 2012-2013. To offset the increase in mandatory spending, it would require taxpayers with modified adjusted gross income in excess of $250,000 to pay self-employment taxes (Social Security and Medicare) on certain income currently exempt from self-employment taxes if that income is received from a professional service partnership or a professional service S corporation in which at least 75% of gross income is attributable to three or fewer shareholders. The offset is estimated to raise $9.0 billion from FY2012 to FY2022.[18]

An S corporation may be subject to the corporate income tax in certain instances. One such instance is the realization of a built-in-gain. A built-in-gain is realized when an S corporation, during the first 10 years of being an S corporation, disposes of an asset that had appreciated in value while the business was organized as a C corporation.[19] The tax rate on a built-in-gain is equal to the highest corporate tax rate (currently 35%). To the extent that built-in-gain exceeds the corporate tax owed on it, the built-in-gain passes through to shareholders who must report it as taxable income. Taxes may also be imposed to recapture previous benefits from the use of investment credits or the last-in-first-out inventory method by the C corporation. Finally, in instances where more than 25% of a converted corporation's gross receipts consist of "passive investment income," a corporate income tax may be imposed. The tax is equal to the highest corporate tax rate and is applied to net income attributable to the excess over 25% of gross receipts. Passive investment income includes such things as dividends, interest, rents, royalties, and capital gains.

Limited Liability Companies

A limited liability company (LLC) combines the favorable tax treatment of a partnership with the limited liability features of a corporation.[20] An LLC, like a partnership, is provided the flexibility to allocate income, losses, deductions, and credits in an amount different than members' ownership interests.[21] The income of a C corporation, on the other hand, is generally distributed to its shareholders in a manner predetermined by rights inherent in each class of stock and the amount of each class of stock a shareholder owns. An S corporation is similarly constrained in the allocation of income, losses, and deductions to its shareholders.

For legal purposes, an LLC, like a corporation, is an entity that is separate from its owners (members). As a result, members are generally provided limited liability protection from the debts of the company. There is no limit to the number of members an LLC may have, unlike with an S corporation. In addition, LLCs are permitted to have multiple classes of ownership interests.

For many years, the IRS had held that any organization would be taxed as a corporation if it had the major characteristics of a corporation. LLCs were designed to lack enough corporate characteristics to avoid such a classification. In most cases, this was accomplished in one of three ways: having the company nominally cease to exist upon the withdrawal of a member; placing restrictions on the transferability of ownership interests; or designating all members as nominal managers.

In 1997, the IRS issued final regulations that in effect allow companies to elect how they will be taxed by simply checking a box on a form.[22] These regulations are typically referred to as "checkthe-box" regulations. A single-owner LLC can elect to be taxed as either a corporation or a sole proprietorship. A multi-owner LLC can elect to be considered either a partnership or an association taxable as a C corporation. These rules apply to any entity that is not otherwise required to file as a corporation or a trust. In general, a business may not change its classification during the 60 months following a check-the-box election.

LLCs are relatively recent creations. Wyoming was the first state to allow LLCs in 1977, followed by Florida in 1982.[23] By the mid-1990s, LLC laws had been enacted in all states.[24]

Tax Treatment of LLCs

The IRC does not contain a section pertaining directly to LLCs. As a result, LLCs must elect to be treated as either a corporation or a partnership.[25] Most LLCs elect to be treated as a partnership and are therefore subject to all of the partnership rules discussed above. In such a case, an LLC is able to achieve the limited liability of a corporation without the double taxation and the restrictions on the pass-through of losses of a C corporation. The members of an LLC may be subject to self-employment taxes, as active partners in a partnership are, but shareholders in an S corporation are not. The ownership interest in most LLCs cannot be traded on a market (otherwise the LLC would be treated as a publicly traded partnership and taxed as a corporation anyway).

Analysis of IRS Business Data

This section analyzes the most recent IRS business data. The analysis begins by summarizing the size of businesses by business type. Because of the delay in the release of certain information, this portion of the analysis is restricted to using data from 2003. Next, a snapshot of how business financial items were distributed across business types in 2006 is provided. The analysis then turns to understanding how businesses have changed over time, particularly between 1980 and 2006. Legislative changes that have affected business decisions are also discussed.

How Big Are Businesses?

A business's size can be measured in a number of ways. Three common measures are a firm's assets, receipts, and number of employees. The Small Business Agency (SBA) uses all three to construct its definition of small business, although assets are normally only considered for financial services/banking firms. Even the SBA, however, does not have a single small business definition. Generally, a firm can have anywhere between 100 and 1500 employees, and between $0.75 million and $35.5 million in average annual receipts and still be considered a small business depending on the industry.

Table 1. Distribution of Businesses Size by Receipts and Type, 2003

Business Type	Number	Less than $250,000	$250,000—$1 million	$1 million—$2.5 million	Greater than $2.5 million
All	27,486,691	87.2%	8.2%	2.5%	2.1%
Sole Proprietorship	19,710,079	96.1%	3.4%	0.4%	0.1%
Partnership	2,375,375	81.9%	10.9%	3.8%	3.5%
S Corporation	3,341,606	59.6%	24.7%	8.7%	6.9%
C Corporation	2,059,631	52.7%	25.0%	11.1%	11.1%

Source: CRS calculations from Internal Revenue Service's Integrated Business Data, http://www.irs.gov/pub/irssoi/03ib01ty.xls.

Table 1 uses business receipts to break down the distribution of businesses according to their size. According to the data, there were roughly 27.5 million businesses operating in the United States in 2003.[26] The overwhelming majority of these businesses were small; at least 87.2%, by the most conservative measure. Most people associate small businesses with pass-throughs and *Table 1* certainly supports this notion. More than 90% of sole proprietorships and partnerships, and more than 80% of S corporations had receipts of less than $1 million. Perhaps less well known is the fact that more than 75% of C corporations also fall under the $1 million threshold. Taken together, the data show that across all forms of organization, most businesses are small.

Still, large firms are responsible for most business activity. *Table 2* summarizes the distribution of business receipts according to business type. The top row, last column of the table shows that a majority of all receipts (78.3%) were generated by businesses with $10 million or more in business receipts. The distribution was particularly skewed for C corporations and partnerships; nearly 90% of C corporation business activity and nearly 80% of partnership business activity occurred among firms with more than $10 million in receipts. The distribution was slightly less skewed for S corporations, although more than half of receipts still accrued to the largest firms. Roughly 78% of sole proprietorship business activity occurred among firms with less than a $1 million in receipts, with slightly under half (49.5%) accruing among firms with less than $250,000 in receipts.

Table 2. Distribution of Receipts By Business Type and Size, 2003

Business Type	Business Receipts	Less than $250,000	$250,000—$1 million	$1 million—$2.5 million	$2.5 million—$10 million	Greater than $10 million
All	$21,860,208,610	3.5%	5.0%	4.8%	13.2%	78.3%
Sole Proprietorship	$1,050,202,446	49.5%	28.2%	10.4%	7.4%	4.5%
Partnership	$2,545,612,266	1.5%	4.0%	4.0%	9.3%	80.3%
C Corporation	$14,112,028,796	0.5%	1.9%	2.6%	5.2%	89.9%
S Corporation	$4,152,365,102	3.3%	10.3%	10.8%	19.1%	56.6%

Source: CRS calculations from Internal Revenue Service's Integrated Business Data, http://www.irs.gov/pub/irssoi/03ib01ty.xls.

Summary of Data in 2006

There were just under 31.8 million businesses in the United States in 2006.[27] *Figure 1* shows that sole proprietorships represented the largest single fraction of businesses (71.6%), followed by S corporations (12.6%), partnerships (9.6%), and C corporations (6.3%). *Figure 1* also makes clear that, as was the case in 2003, the distribution of business receipts tended to be concentrated among C corporations. So too was the distribution of business income and business deductions claimed. For example, C corporations generated 62.5% of business receipts, 48.4% of net business income, and claimed 66.3% of all business deductions, while only accounting for 6.3% of all businesses. Sole proprietorships, partnerships, and S corporations collectively generated 37.5% of business receipts and 51.6% of business income, while claiming 37.5% of business deductions.

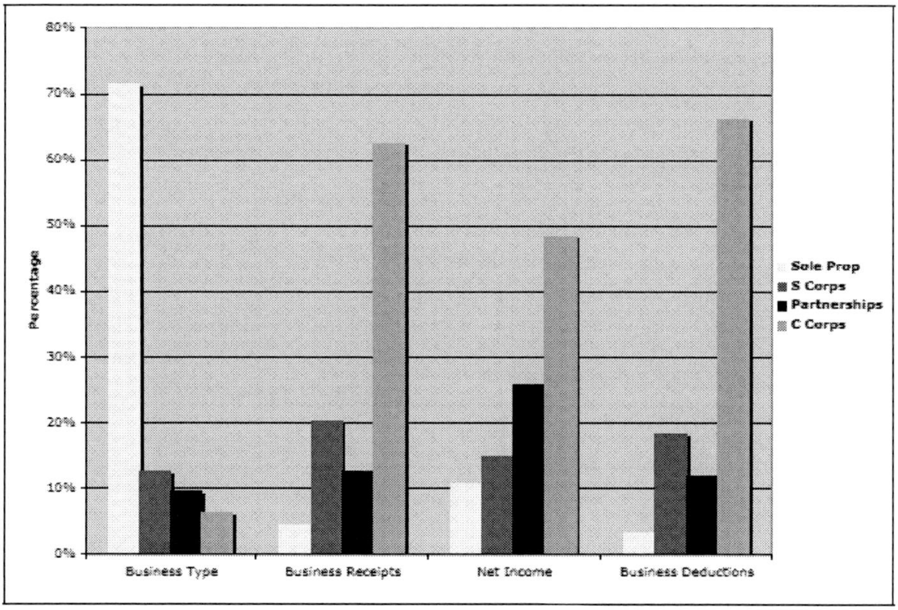

Source: CRS calculations from Internal Revenue Service's Business Tax Statistics, various tables, http://www.irs.gov/taxstats/bustaxstats/index.html.
Note: Net income is measured as net income less deficit.

Figure 1. Distribution of Business Types and Business Financial Items in 2006.

Distribution of Business Data Over Time

The distribution of businesses has changed somewhat over time. *Figure 2* shows that in 1980 the majority of businesses in the United States were organized as sole proprietorships, followed by C corporations, partnerships, and finally S corporations. *Figure 2* also shows that while the sole proprietorship still remained the most popular form of organization in 2006, the fraction of businesses organized as C corporations had been reduced by more than half, from 16.6% to 6.3%. At the same time, the fraction of businesses choosing to organize as an S corporation tripled over the 1980-2006 period, increasing from 4.2% to 12.6%. The number of partnerships fell slightly since 1980, leading S corporations to eventually outnumber partnerships.

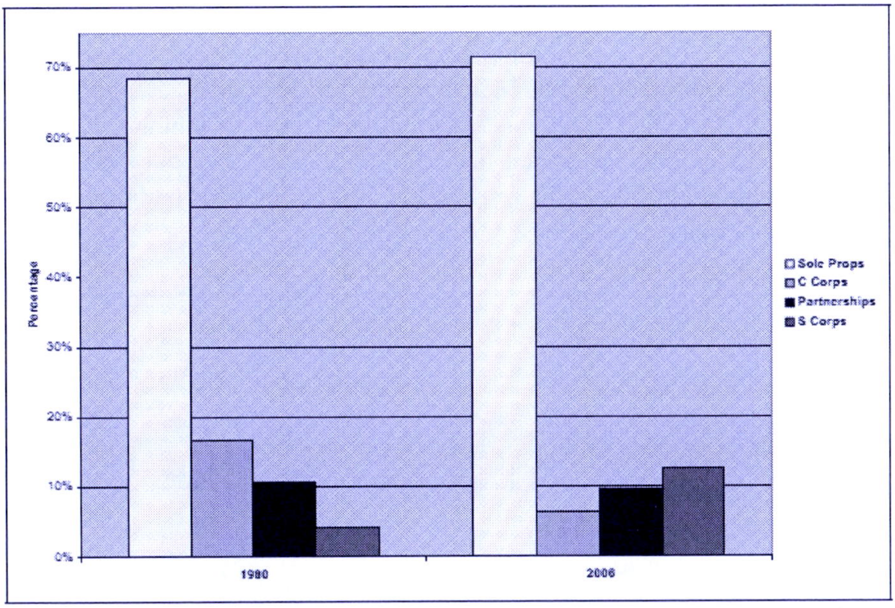

Source: CRS calculations from Internal Revenue Service's Business Tax Statistics, various tables, http://www.irs.gov/taxstats/bustaxstats/index.html.

Figure 2. Distribution of Business Types in 1980 and 2006.

Some of the trend away from C corporations and partnerships in favor of S corporations may be attributed to a number of legislative changes that occurred in the mid-1980s. The Tax Reform Act of 1986 (TRA86; P.L. 99-514), which implemented broad changes to the tax code, increased the appeal of being taxed under the individual income tax rather than the corporate income tax. Prior to TRA86, the highest individual income tax rate was 50%, whereas the highest corporate income tax rate was 46%. TRA86 eventually lowered the highest individual tax rate to 28% and the highest corporate tax rate to 34%. An IRS study found that the more favorable tax treatment under the individual tax schedule after TRA86 induced certain businesses organized as C corporations to reorganize as S corporations.[28] In-line with this explanation, *Figure 3* shows a distinct movement away from C corporations in favor of S corporations in the years immediately following the enactment of TRA86.

Figure 3 also displays a downward trend in the fraction of businesses that chose to organize as partnerships beginning after TRA86. Until 1986, partnerships had been popular among some taxpayers because of the opportunity they presented to claim tax credits and deductions generated by the partnership with little or no active engagement in the partnership's operation. As a result, some partnerships were viewed as "tax shelters" with few benefits beyond reducing its members' tax liability. In an attempt to curb the use of tax shelters, TRA86 instituted limitations on the amount of credits and deductions passive investment partners could claim to reduce their non-passive income tax liability. As a result, the attractiveness of partnerships for such taxpayers was reduced.

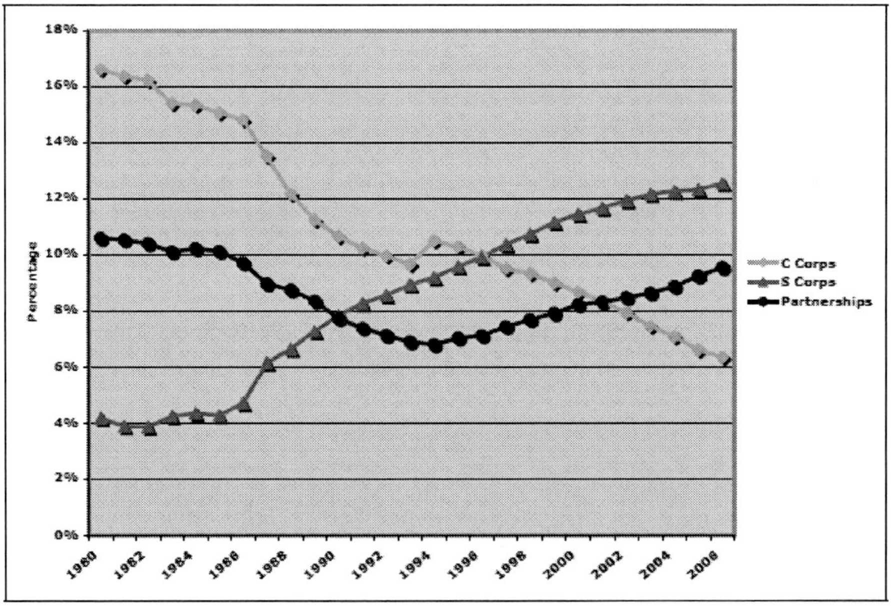

Source: CRS calculations from Internal Revenue Service's Business Tax Statistics, various tables, http://www.irs.gov/taxstats/bustaxstats/index.html.

Note: Sole proprietorships are excluded from the figure because they remained a relatively constant fraction of all businesses at around 70%.

Figure 3. Distribution of C Corporations, S Corporations, and Partnerships, 1980-2006.

Legislative changes throughout the 1990s continued to impact businesses. By 1993, the more favorable treatment previously afforded business income under the individual tax system had disappeared as the Omnibus Budget Reconciliation Act of 1990 (P.L. 101-508) and the Omnibus Budget Reconciliation Act of 1993 (P.L. 103-66) eventually pushed the top individual tax rate above the top corporate tax rate. Although there was a temporary increase in the percentage of C corporations around this time, it did not appear to greatly affect the number of S corporations, which continued to increase in popularity.

Figure 3 shows that there was also renewed popularity in partnerships that began in the mid-1990s. LLCs, many of which elect to be treated as partnerships for tax purposes, appeared on the partnership tax form for the first time in 1993. Between 1993 and 2006, partnerships have grown 38%, with most of this growth being attributed to the increase in LLCs.

S corporations also continued to grow in popularity during the 1990s and the early part of this decade, due in part to an expansion in the shareholder limit.

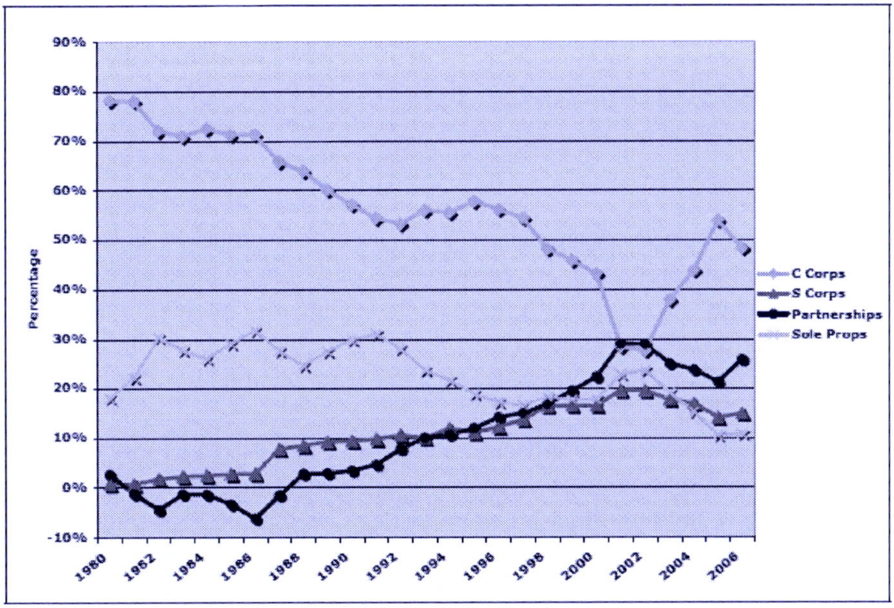

Source: CRS calculations from Internal Revenue Service's Integrated Business Data, Table 1, http://www.irs.gov/pub/irs-soi/80ot1all.xls.

Notes: Net income is measured as net income less deficit. This measure of income is different than taxable business income, although the two will generally be close.

Figure 4. Distribution of Net Business Income, 1980-2006.

The Small Business Job Protection Act of 1996 (SBJPA; P.L. 104-188) raised the shareholder limit from 35 to 75. In 2005, the shareholder limit was raised to 100 as part of the American Jobs Creation Act of 2004 (P.L. 108-357). The effect was to allow S corporations to access larger capital pools and expand in size without needing to reorganize as a C corporation or LLC.

As the distribution of business types has changed so has the distribution of business income. In 1980, C corporations generated nearly 80% of all business profits in the United States (*Figure 4*), while representing just under 17% of all businesses (see *Figure 2).* By 2006, however, C corporations were responsible for slightly less than 50% of all business profits, although this number had fallen to as low as 28% in 2002. The fraction of income generated by sole proprietorships was generally stable until the early 1990s, at which point it began a slight trend downward. The fraction of income being generated by partnerships and S corporations grew steadily for most of the time period. However, the fraction of income attributable to these two business forms has fallen somewhat recently due to the surge in C corporate income.

APPENDIX. ADDITIONAL FORMS OF ORGANIZATION

RICs

Regulated investment companies (RICs), most of which are mutual funds or venture capital companies, are corporations or associations that invest their members' money in securities and pass the dividends, interest, and capital gains through to their investors. If they meet the requirements of IRC Sections 851-855, the amounts distributed to investors are not subject to the corporate income tax.

According to the IRC, a RIC must derive at least 90% of its gross income from dividends, interest, gains from the sale of securities, and other income from handling or holding of cash and securities (foreign currency transactions, loans of securities, etc.). At least 50% of its assets must be invested in securities and cash, and no more than 25% can be invested in the securities of one issuer. Except for certified venture capital companies, the company may not own more than 10% of the voting stock of another corporation.

RICs are subject to corporate income tax on undistributed taxable income less capital gains. However, if a RIC distributes each year at least 90% of its income (excluding capital gains) to shareholders as dividends, the amounts distributed are deductible. In fact, almost all mutual funds distribute all of their income (by crediting it to shareholders' accounts) and so pay no corporate income tax. The shareholders include the dividends credited to them in their own incomes and are liable for any tax the dividend income generates.

Capital gains on the company's securities trades are accounted for separately and are paid out to shareholders as capital gains dividends. Capital gains dividends are treated by the shareholder as long-term capital gains. Because a mutual fund's trading activity can generate capital gains even when its own shares have lost value, shareholders can have taxable capital gain dividends in a year when their overall investments in the fund have fallen in value. They cannot net the unrealized loss on their mutual fund shares against their capital gains dividends, which represent realized capital gains.

RICs have the option of retaining capital gains and paying the corporate capital gains tax on them. In this case, the gains are allocated to the shareholders as if paid out in dividends and included in the shareholder's income. However, shareholders are allowed a credit for their share of tax paid by the RIC.

REITs

A real estate investment trust (REIT) is a domestic corporation, trust, or association with at least 100 shareholders that elects to be taxed as a REIT and meets the requirements of IRC Sections 856-859. According to the IRC, a REIT must derive at least 95% of its gross income from dividends, interest, capital gains, and qualified real estate income, and at least 75% of its gross income from real estate rents, mortgage interest, sales of real estate and mortgages, and other income related to real estate, including income from foreclosure property. The REIT must not directly perform management or other services for its rental properties. At least 75% of the REIT's assets must consist of real estate and mortgages, cash and cash items, and government securities.

The taxation of a REIT and its shareholders—the IRC calls them "beneficiaries"—is similar to that of a RIC. If the REIT distributes at least 90% (95% before 2001) of its net income to shareholders, it is not subject to corporate taxation on the amounts distributed, which are taxed at the shareholder level. As with RICs, capital gains are accounted for separately and are considered long-term gain when distributed to shareholders. REITs may also elect to retain capital gains and pay a tax at the corporate level, which is then passed on to shareholders as a credit. Like RICs, the majority of REITs distribute all of their income to escape corporate taxation.

Trusts

Trusts are entities that hold title to property for other persons; they are not supposed to be associations or conduct business (IRS Regulation 301.7701-1). They either distribute or credit their income to beneficiaries, who are taxable on it, or pay a tax themselves under a special individual income tax rate schedule (IRC Section 1(e)). There are many kinds of trusts and extensive tax rules to govern them (IRC Subchapter J). (The word "trust" is used in the IRC for many dissimilar entities, some of which are taxed as corporations.)

REMICs

Real estate mortgage investment conduits, or REMICs, are pools of mortgages that sell shares to investors and pass the mortgage interest income through to the investors. Investors holding "regular interests" receive fixed payments, deductible by the REMIC and taxable as interest income to the investor.

"Residual interest" holders are allocated a pro-rata share of the remaining income, taxable to them as ordinary income. The REMIC is not allowed to trade in mortgages; such activity would be a "prohibited transaction" and taxed at 100% of any gain. (IRC Section 860A-860G)

FASITs

Financial asset securitization investment trusts, or FASITS, are entities owned by C corporations and used to hold the C corporation's securitized credit card receivables, auto loans, home equity loans, and other consumer debt.

Their operation is similar to a REMIC, with "regular interests" receiving fixed payments taxable as interest income and the "ownership interest" (the C corporation) receiving the remainder as taxable income. "Prohibited transactions," including trading securities and receiving income from any other assets, are taxed at 100% of any gain. (IRC Section 860L)

End Notes

[1] Sole proprietorships and single member limited liability corporations are technically disregarded entities. As the first paragraph notes, economists usually group these business types in with the pass-through businesses. For a disregarded entity there is no entity level tax return. All income is reported on the individual's personal tax return, aggregated with other income, and taxed according to individual tax rates.

[2] Congressional Budget Office and staff of the Joint Committee on Taxation, Estimate of Budgetary Effects of S. 2343, the Stop the Student Loan Interest Rate Hike Act of 2012, as Introduced on April 24, 2012, prepared, 112th Cong., 2nd sess., April 25, 2012, http://www.cbo.gov/sites/default/files/cbofiles/attachments/s2343.pdf.

[3] There are several other, less prevalent, forms of organization available to businesses including cooperatives, mutual organizations, credit unions, trusts, and estates.

[4] 26 U.S.C. §7701(a)(2) defines a partnership as "a syndicate, group, pool, joint venture, or other unincorporated organization, through or by means of which any business, financial operation, or venture is carried on, and which is not, within the meaning of this title, a trust or estate or a corporation."

[5] While important, a partnership agreement is not legally required. In its absence either the Uniform Partnership Act (UPA) or the Revised Uniform Partnership Act (RUPA) would provide default rules. UPA was adopted by all states, while RUPA has been adopted by many, but not yet all. Where adopted, RUPA would apply if there were no partnership agreement.

[6] John E. Moye, The Law of Business Organizations (NY: West Legal Studies, 2004), p. 57.

[7] Kenneth E. Anderson, Thomas R. Pope, and John L. Kramer, et al., Federal Taxation 2004: Corporations, Partnerships, Estates, and Trusts (Upper Saddle River, NG: Prentice Hall, 2004), pp. D-6.

[8] Partners may be jointly and severally liable (if RUPA is applicable) or equally liable (if UPA is applicable).

[9] In some cases, a tax matters partner is named.

[10] William H. Hoffman, William A. Raabe, and James E. Smith, et al., Corporations, Partnerships, Estates, and Trusts, ed. 2003 (Thomson Southwestern, 2003), pp. 10-4.

[11] See 26 U.S.C. §7704(c).

[12] See 26 U.S.C. §7704(g).

[13] See 26 U.S.C. §772 for a detailed list.

[14] Except large oil and gas partnerships, which must continue to report depletion and intangible drilling costs under the old rules for some partners.

[15] While a business may choose any state in which to incorporate, Delaware is by far the most popular. According to Delaware's Division of Corporations, 63% of Fortune 500 companies chose Delaware as their state of incorporation. See http://corp.delaware.gov/.

[16] Shareholders may, however, have different voting rights.

[17] Internal Revenue Service, Paying Reasonable Compensation to the S Corporation Shareholder-Employee, Stakeholder Headliners, vol. 32, Washington, DC, December 10, 2002.

[18] Congressional Budget Office and staff of the Joint Committee on Taxation, Estimate of Budgetary Effects of S. 2343, the Stop the Student Loan Interest Rate Hike Act of 2012, as Introduced on April 24, 2012, prepared, 112th Cong., 2nd sess., April 25, 2012, http://www.cbo.gov/sites/default/files/cbofiles/attachments/s2343.pdf.

[19] The American Recovery and Reinvestment Act of 2009 (P.L. 111-5) reduced the 10-year realization period to 7 years for gains recognized in 2009 and 2010.

[20] John E. Moye, The Law of Business Organizations, 6th ed. (Clifton Park, NY: Thomson Delmar Learning, 2004), p. 121.

[21] The owners of an LLC are referred to as "members."

[22] Treas. Reg. §301.7701-3.

[23] Larry E. Ribstein, "The Emergence Of The Limited Liability Company," The Business Lawyer, November 1995, p. 1.

[24] Paul A. McDaniel, Martin J. McMahon, and Daniel L. Simmons, Federal Income Taxation of Business Organizations, 3rd ed. (New York: Foundation Press, 1999), p. 8.

[25] Single-member LLCs must elect to be treated as either a corporation or a sole proprietorship.

[26] This figure excludes farm sole proprietorships.

[27] CRS calculations for the IRS's Business Tax Statistics, various tables.

[28] Susan M. Whittman and Amy Gill, "S Corporation Elections After the Tax Reform Act of 1986," SOI Bulletin, publication 1136 (Spring 1998).

In: Business Taxation
Editors: J. C. Teague and K. Fawner
ISBN: 978-1-62257-998-3

Chapter 2

FEDERAL BUSINESS TAXATION: THE CURRENT SYSTEM, ITS EFFECTS, AND OPTIONS FOR REFORM*

Donald J. Marples

SUMMARY

A foundation of the broad tax revisions implemented 24 years ago by the Tax Reform Act of 1986 was tax "neutrality"—the idea that economic efficiency and economic welfare are promoted if the distorting impact of taxes on business and other economic decisions is minimized. Based on this principle, the 1986 act broadened the tax base and reduced statutory tax rates set forth by the tax code. In time, however, the underlying thrust of tax policy has changed. Rather than neutrality and efficiency, recent business tax legislation has been guided more by a concern for promoting investment and capital formation, and by attention to the perceived impact of taxes on the ability of U.S. firms to compete with foreign companies. Further, recent interest in fundamental tax reform has been partly stimulated by these same concerns for capital formation and competitiveness.

Twenty-four years after the 1986 act, business tax policy is thus potentially at a crossroads, and it is useful to take stock of where the system stands, the economic effects it is known to have, and the principal

---

* This is an edited, reformatted and augmented version of Congressional Research Services publication RL33171, dated September 9, 2010.

options for reform. Several data series show a similar pattern in the level of corporate taxes: corporate income taxes have generally declined over the post-World War II period. At the same time, however, significant disparities in the structure of business taxes have remained, suggesting a persistence of distortions caused by the tax system: corporate-sector investment remains heavily taxed compared to non-corporate business and owner-occupied housing; debt is favored over equity; and equipment is favored over structures.

The base of business taxation is the return to business investment; business taxes thus influence the economy through their impact on investment. In broad terms, business taxes can, at least in principle, reduce capital formation and thus impair long-term economic growth by making saving and investment less attractive. This effect, however, depends on a robust saving response to taxes, the presence of which is uncertain. Another impact is on the allocation of investment among different sectors and asset types. Here, business taxes likely distort investment decisions, reducing economic efficiency and economic welfare. In the case of equity, economic theory suggests that in the long run, the burden of business taxation is shared among all owners of capital and has a progressive effect on the tax system.

Various hypothetical alternatives exist for reforming the business tax system. One possibility is to move in the direction of the 1986 Tax Reform Act by broadening the existing tax base—that is, by eliminating tax benefits and preferences. Another possibility—and one that is favored by many economists—is to adopt some form of tax integration that would eliminate the double taxation of corporate income. A third option is to adopt a form of consumption tax, under which new business investment would be exempt from tax. Either corporate tax integration or a consumption tax could improve economic efficiency, but only if the design were to avoid the types of distortions present in the current system.

INTRODUCTION

Twenty-four years ago, the broad tax revisions implemented by the Tax Reform Act of 1986 (P.L. 99-514) were based on tax "neutrality"—the idea that economic efficiency and economic welfare are promoted if the distorting impact of taxes on business and other economic decisions is minimized. To this end, the 1986 act broadened the tax base for both businesses and individuals, scaling back various narrowly-applicable tax preferences and benefits, and reduced the statutory tax rate.

In time, however, the general thrust of business-tax policy began to change, and in recent years policy has been guided more by a concern for the level of investment and capital formation, as well as the perceived impact of taxes on U.S. competitiveness. Thus, measures designed to promote tax-consistency across investments and activities have been supplanted by provisions designed to stimulate investment and assist in the ability of U.S. firms to compete with foreign companies. Cases in point are the temporary "bonus depreciation" provisions enacted in 2002 and 2003 and the broad tax deduction for domestic production included in the omnibus business-tax bill passed in 2004.[1] At the same time, there has recently been renewed congressional and public interest in broad reform of the U.S. tax system. In contrast to 1986, however, much of the recent interest in reform has centered on a shift in the tax base to consumption rather than a comprehensive measure of income—a change in focus that is based, in part, on the same concerns for capital formation and competitiveness that underlie much of recent business-tax legislation.

Twenty-four years after the 1986 act, business taxation is thus potentially at a crossroads. Will the thrust of tax policy continue to shift away from the principles of efficiency and neutrality that guided tax reform two decades in the past? If fundamental tax reform is adopted in the near future, would it include a revamped system of business taxation? If so, what would business taxation look like? Regardless of the outcome, it is useful at this point to take stock, to pause and review the current system and its effects. The charts and discussions on the following pages are intended to assist in that exercise. The report begins with a discussion of the principal economic effects of business taxation. Its concluding sections review the various theoretical principles on which fundamental reform of business taxation might be based.

BASIC STRUCTURE OF THE CURRENT SYSTEM

Businesses can take a variety of forms, ranging from large, publicly held corporations, to more closely held corporations, to partnerships (large and small), to firms that are run by only a single self-employed owner. With some exceptions, the rules for determining taxable income—for example, how to calculate depreciation and other deductions—are the same, regardless of the type of business. The particular manner in which that income is taxed, however, does vary, depending on the type of business.

Income earned by large, publicly held corporations ("C" corporations, in tax parlance) is generally subject to the corporate income tax—one of the principal structural components of the federal tax system, along with the individual income tax, the estate and gift tax, excise taxes, and social security taxes. In conceptual terms, the present U.S. corporate income tax is sometimes described as a "classical" system that applies as though corporations were entities with an existence separate from their owners, the stockholders. The tax applies to taxable corporate income, corporate profits (after deducting interest) as defined by the tax code. It applies separately and in addition to the individual income tax's applicability to shareholder's dividends and capital gains. As discussed in more detail below (see the section on the economic effects of the tax), this means that income subject to the corporate income tax is generally taxed twice— once under the corporate income tax in the hands of corporations, and once under the individual income tax when stockholders receive dividends or realize capital gains. The double taxation does not occur, however, in the case of corporate income generated by debt-financed investment, since the return to such investment is paid to creditors as interest and is tax-deductible. Double taxation also does not apply in the case of income paid to tax-exempt stockholders—for example, pension funds.

Income earned by relatively closely held corporations—termed "S corporations" by the tax code—is not subject to the corporate income tax and so also is not taxed twice. Instead, an S corporation's income is "passed through" to the firm's stockholders and taxed to them under the individual income tax, regardless of whether the income is actually distributed. To qualify as an S corporation, a firm can have no more than 100 shareholders and must meet certain other requirements.

As with S-corporation profits, partnership taxable income is not subject to an entity-level tax such as the corporate income tax. Instead, each partner is taxed under the individual income tax on his or her share of the partnership's profit.[2] Individual income taxes also apply to business income earned by self-employed persons who operate sole proprietorships. As with partnerships and S corporations, no separate tax is applied at the entity (i.e., business) level.

According to estimates by the Congressional Budget Office, 62% of tangible business assets are owned by C corporations; the remainder (38%) is owned by other business entities (i.e., partnerships, sole proprietorships, and S corporations).[3]

As noted above, rules for determining taxable income are generally the same, regardless of the form of business organization.[4] The base of federal business income taxes is generally profits, net of interest payments. Profits, in turn, are gross receipts—for example, sales—minus deductible costs. Important categories of deductible costs include interest payments, wages, purchased materials and other inputs, and a depreciation allowance for the decline in value of tangible capital. Importantly, the tax code's definition of these elements frequently differs from how an economist or accountant might define them. For example, the tax code may fully or partly exempt certain types of income from inclusion in taxable income—a specific example is the partial deduction the tax code permits for income from domestic production activities. Or, the tax code may require the recognition of income at a different point in time than when economic theory indicates it is actually earned or permit a deduction to be claimed at a different time from when the cost is actually incurred. Regardless of the underlying provision, instances where taxable income differs from economic income can provide either a tax benefit or tax penalty and (as described more fully below) influence how the economy's capital resources are allocated.

U.S. firms increasingly participate in international markets, and so an overview of the U.S. structure would be incomplete without including its international dimension. In the international context, the U.S. applies what is sometimes termed a "residence" based tax system, but with important exceptions. The United States generally applies its corporate income to the worldwide income of corporations chartered in (i.e., "resident" in) the United States. At the same time, however, U.S. firms can generally indefinitely postpone (defer) U.S. tax on foreign-source income as long as the income is earned by foreign-chartered subsidiary corporations and reinvested abroad. To alleviate double taxation, the United States permits its taxpayers to credit foreign taxes they pay against U.S. taxes they would otherwise owe, subject to the limitation that foreign taxes can only be credited against U.S. foreign- (and not U.S.-) source income Foreign businesses in the United States are generally subject to U.S. business taxes on their U.S.- source income. If a foreign firm operates in the United States through a U.S.-chartered subsidiary corporation, the subsidiary is generally subject to U.S. tax in its role as a resident U.S. corporation; like other U.S.-chartered corporations, it is subject to U.S. tax on its worldwide income, regardless of the nationality of its owner(s). If, on the other hand, the foreign firm operates in the United States through a branch of the foreign-chartered parent corporation, the foreign firm is subject to U.S. tax on its income from U.S., but not foreign, sources; the United States taxes foreign persons and corporations on their income from the active conduct of a U.S. trade or business. (The economic effects of international aspects of the federal tax system are discussed below.)

Another structural component of the system is the alternative minimum tax (AMT). The tax code provides both a corporate AMT and an individual AMT; a business may be subject to either, depending on whether it pays the corporate income tax or is taxed under the individual income tax as a sole proprietorship or passthrough entity. Both AMTs essentially require a taxpayer to pay either the regular tax or the AMT, whichever is higher. The two liabilities will ordinarily differ for a business because they are computed differently. The AMT is imposed at a lower statutory rate than the regular tax, and the base of the AMT is more inclusive than that of the regular tax, permitting fewer omissions and tax benefits. The purpose of the AMT is to ensure that few truly profitable corporations escape paying at least some tax.

The importance of the AMT in the structure is difficult to quantify. Recent data on the share of corporate investment subject to the tax are not available. The numbers that are available show that prior to 1999, the AMT was important: in 1998, more than one-quarter of corporate assets were held by firms paying the AMT, and within the manufacturing sector over one-half of firms were AMT firms. Beginning in 1999, however, new, more generous AMT depreciation rules likely reduced the portion of investment affected by the AMT.

Level of Corporate Taxes, Past and Present

The level of corporate tax receipts has fluctuated over time. This review of the data focuses primarily on the corporate income tax; there are a variety of ways to gauge its size. First, the general importance of the tax in terms of any economic effects it has can be assessed by looking at the level of the tax compared to the size of the economy—that is, by assessing corporate tax revenue as a percent of gross domestic product (GDP). Figure 1, below, presents such data for fiscal years 1934 to 2009, thus showing the position of corporate revenues from well before World War II to the latest year available. Clearly, the chart shows that corporate tax revenues have declined from their peak during World War II (7% in FY1945) and from another peak that coincided with the Korean War (6.1% in FY1952). The chart also shows that they have declined from what might be termed an intermediate level of between 2% and 4% in the 1960s and 1970s to a level between 1% and 2% in recent years, but with an "uptick" beginning in 2005 before falling dramatically in 2009.

While corporate taxes have declined as a percentage of GDP, Figure 2, below, shows that corporate income-tax revenue likewise declined as a share of total federal revenue, and in roughly the same pattern. Corporate tax revenue's share of total federal revenue declined from a peak of 40% during World War II (FY1943), and a somewhat lower peak of 32% during the Korean War (FY1952), to levels of slightly above and below 10% after the late 1980s. Again, there was a surge beginning in 2005 before falling dramatically in 2009.

Source: U.S. Office of Management and Budget, *Historical Tables: Budget of the United States, Fiscal Year 2011* (Washington: GPO, 2010).

Figure 1. Corporate Taxes as a Percentage of GDP, FY1934-FY2009.

These broad measures of corporate taxes are useful as rough indicators of how the level of corporate taxes in the economy has changed, but lack precision in showing the burden of corporate taxes and the causes of the taxes' fluctuations. For example, a decline in the share of national income comprising corporate profits is partly responsible for the reductions shown in Figures 1 and 2. Figure 3 corrects for this with a series that holds profits constant. It shows average effective corporate tax rates (AETRs), which are the ratio of federal corporate income taxes to before-tax corporate profits. According to the AETRs, the aggregate burden of corporate taxes steadily declined during the 1960s and 1970s, reaching a low of about 20% of corporate profits during the early 1980s before rising to a plateau of around 25% that has generally prevailed from 1986 to the present. The anomalous year in the last two decades was 2000, which registered a spike in the AETR to 34%.

Source: U.S. Office of Management and Budget, *Historical Tables: Budget of the United States, Fiscal Year 2011* (Washington: GPO, 2010).

Figure 2. Corporate Tax Revenue as a Percentage of Total Federal Tax Revenue, FY1934-FY2009.

Since AETRs hold the level of corporate profits constant, a principal determinant of variations in the rates is legislated changes, and several can be linked to the fluctuations in the AETRS. At least three factors are likely responsible for the decline in rates during the 1960s, 1970s, and early 1980s. First, during the 1970s and 1980s, several reductions in the statutory corporate tax rate that applies to taxable income were enacted. Second, while taxable corporate profits were artificially inflated during the 1970s by a rising price level, firms were also permitted to claim investment tax credits. Third, the Economic Recovery Tax Act of 1981 provided accelerated depreciation deductions, which likely played a prominent role in the sharp drop in tax rates in the early 1980s. Following the reduction, rates increased again in the mid-1980s. Part of the increase was likely due to timing results from the 1981 act, but the Tax Reform Act of 1986 was also likely responsible for part of the increase. The act reduced statutory tax rates, but also repealed the investment credit and scaled back depreciation allowances.

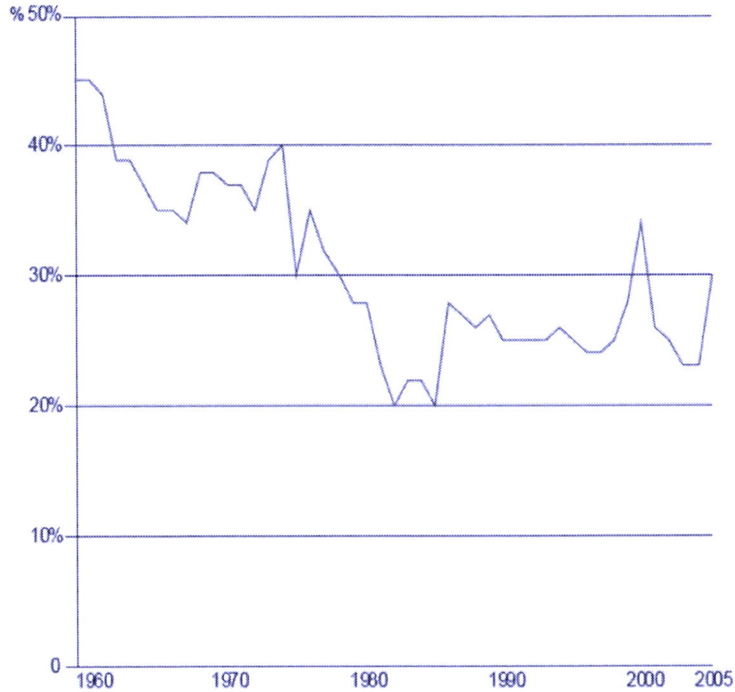

Source: CRS Report RL30469, Average Effective Corporate Tax Rates: 1959 to 2005, by Steven Maguire.

Figure 3. Average Effective Corporate Tax Rates: Federal Corporate Taxes as a Percentage of Corporate Profits, FY1959-FY2005.

AETRs have their own shortcoming as a gauge of the corporate tax burden. They provide only one-year snapshots of a firm's tax burden, while according to economic theory, taxes impose a burden on capital income by reducing the expected rate of return over the life of new investment. For example, the tax burden on an investment consists not only of taxes paid in its first year, but also those paid in, say, the fifth year of its life. In addition, because of discounting, the tax burden on investment depends partly on how taxes are distributed over an investment's life; a given amount of taxes matters more to a firm the sooner it is paid. The same is true of deductions, but in reverse; a given deduction is more valuable the sooner it is claimed.

"Marginal" effective tax rates (METRs) take these factors into account, measuring the impact of taxes over a representative investment's entire lifetime as well as the timing of payments and deductions. Unlike AETRs, METRs can thus accurately register the impact of provisions such as accelerated depreciation, whose value depends crucially on timing. METRs also take into account the interaction of inflation and tax rules, statutory tax rates, and investment subsidies such as the investment tax credit. In general, a marginal effective tax rate is the difference between the pretax and after-tax return on prospective investment, divided by the pre-tax return.[5]

Figure 4, below, presents a set of METRs for the period 1953 through 2005. The top line in the figure shows METRs for corporate investment. The second line is rates for non-corporate business and moves in tandem with corporate rates, but at a lower level. (The third line is the METR for the remaining broad category of capital investment: owner-occupied housing.) The series shows a decline in rates from the early 1950s to the mid-1960s—the result of accelerated depreciation, introduction of an investment tax credit, and reduced statutory tax rates. Rates then rose in the late 1960s and varied during the 1970s, a consequence of repeal and reintroduction of the investment tax credit as well as inflation. Rates declined sharply in 1981, reflecting the Economic Recovery Tax Act's accelerated depreciation provisions. METRs then remained relatively stable until 2001 to 2003, when reductions in shareholder-level taxes (including reduced tax rates on capital gains and dividends) as well as bonus depreciation caused a reduction in effective rates. Rates picked up again in 2005, with the expiration of bonus depreciation.[6]

The preceding charts show four different measures of corporate taxes: taxes as a share of GDP, corporate tax revenues as a percentage of federal revenue, average effective corporate tax rates, and marginal effective tax rates. Each series shows the same general pattern in the period after World War II: a general decline in the level of corporate taxes. But before accepting this broad pattern as the conclusion of this look at corporate tax data, note the relative position of the three lines in Figure 4, denoting METRs for corporate investment, for non-corporate business, and for owner-occupied housing. In contrast to the general direction of each set of METRs—they have all declined, showing a decline in capital taxes in general—their relative position has remained the same. And importantly, it is the relative tax treatment of investment that affects the allocation of investment among different uses, and differences in the treatment of different investments that distort the allocation of capital. Thus, to the conclusion that business taxes have generally declined in the post-World War II period, there is an additional important result:

corporate investment remains relatively heavily taxed compared to non-corporate business and (especially) owner-occupied housing.[7] The report's next section explores the implications of this result by discussing the economic effects of business taxes.

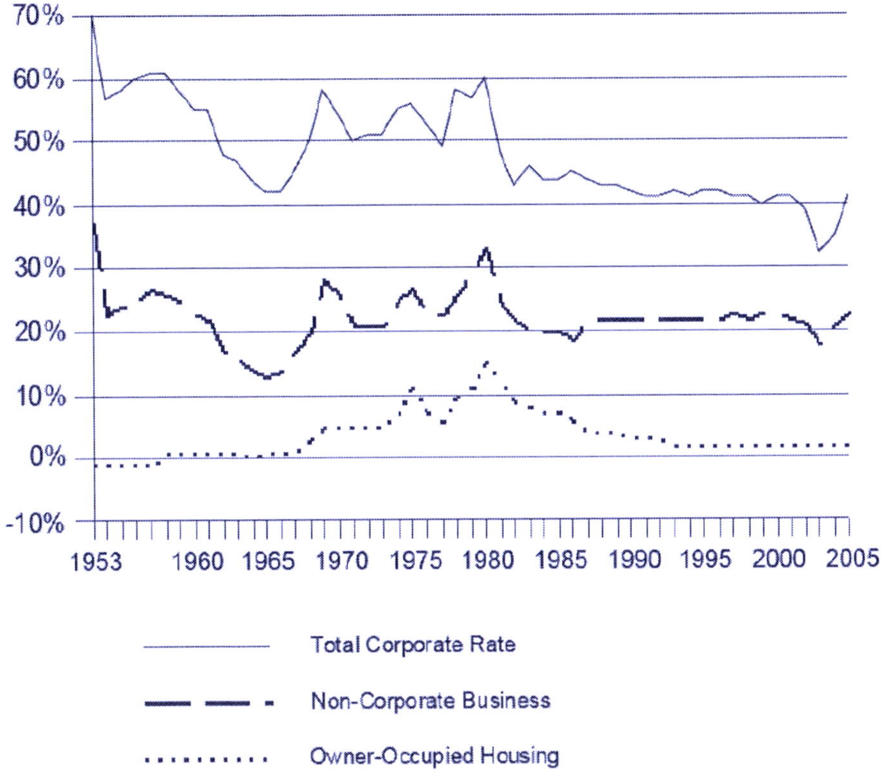

Source: CRS Report RS21706, Historical Effective Marginal Tax Rates on Capital Income, by Jane G. Gravelle.

Figure 4. Marginal Effective Tax Rates on Corporate and Other Investment, FY1953-FY2005.

ECONOMIC EFFECTS OF BUSINESS TAXES

The base of the corporate income tax and of business taxes in general is income from capital investment. It is thus not surprising that business taxes exert their most direct effects through their impact on the return to new investment. By reducing the return to capital investment, business taxes—at least in principle—can affect the economy's commitment of resources to capital formation in general, although this effect may be muted. Business taxes can also affect the allocation of investment funds among different sectors, as suggested at the end of the preceding section. And while businesses are not people, the burden of business taxes is ultimately borne by individuals; business taxes thus have an impact on the fairness of the tax system.

Business Taxes and Capital Formation

Because they apply to the return on investment, business taxes can potentially reduce the economy's overall level of investment and its stock of capital. There are indeed some who advocate cutting business taxes as a means of boosting capital formation: according to economic theory, an increase in the capital stock boosts long run growth, which, in turn, increases living standards and per capita income in the future.[8]

Yet business taxes do not necessarily have a pronounced effect on the aggregate level of capital in the economy. A key element is the economy's supply of saving, and there are indications that individual savers may not respond robustly to tax cuts by increasing their saving. Note first, however, that business taxes do likely have an impact on firms' investment demand. Taxes on business profits increase the rate of return a given asset must earn, before taxes, in order to generate the rate of return required to attract funds from savers. A tax on business investment thus encourages firms to forgo a range of less profitable investments they might otherwise undertake. And indeed, as described below, uneven application of business taxes results in less investment in heavily taxed areas and more investment in lightly taxed projects.

But investment demand is just one side of the market for capital; the other side is household saving. And if individual saving is unresponsive to changes in the after-tax rate of return, then changes in investment demand will have little impact on the overall stock of capital: boosts in demand will principally serve to increase the economy's real interest rate. For example, provision of a tax credit for businesses to undertake investment may indeed boost business demand for the particular type of investment in question, and firms may boost the rate of return they are willing to pay savers for each quantity of investment. But unless savers are willing to increase the quantity of funds they supply in response to the higher return, there will be no increase in the capital stock.

Economic theory provides no unambiguous answer on how saving responds to its rate of return, after taxes, and is subject to countervailing effects. In isolation, a tax on investment income—that is, on saving—reduces the price of current consumption compared to future consumption, and may thus reduce saving. On the other hand, a tax on saving increases the amount of saving an individual must undertake before taxes in order to achieve a particular dollar amount, after taxes, and may thus increase saving. The answer to the question therefore depends on the empirical evidence. And while there have been numerous econometric studies of saving, their results differ.[9] This has led some to suggest that instead of providing tax incentives for saving and investment, a more certain approach to boosting aggregate national saving would be reducing government dissaving by reducing the government's budget deficit.[10]

Business Taxes and Economic Efficiency

Not only does the amount of capital matter for economic performance, but so too does how that capital is employed. And while business taxes likely have little impact on long-run growth and capital formation, they do affect the allocation of investment among different uses and thus affect economic efficiency. Because taxes affect investment demand, they distort the allocation of investment where they apply unevenly, channeling funds to tax-favored assets and away from more heavily taxed assets. The results for economic efficiency follow: economic theory indicates that undistorted market prices and investment returns generally allocate resources to their most productive use so that capital and other resources produce the mix of output that consumers value most, and economic welfare is maximized. To the extent business taxes distort the allocation of resources, they reduce economic welfare.

One prominent distortion posed by the U.S. tax system results from the double-taxation of corporate-source equity income—its taxation under both the corporate income tax and the individual income tax. As a result, investment is channeled away from the corporate sector into less heavily taxed areas such as owner-occupied housing and non-corporate business (see the effective tax rates in Figure 4, above). A second distortion posed by the corporate income tax is its favoring of debt over equity in the financing of investment. The return to debt-financed investment consists of corporate interest payments to creditors; the return to equity consists of dividends and capital gains. Since interest is tax-deductible at the corporate level but dividends and capital gains are not, firms are encouraged to use higher levels of debt than they otherwise would, increasing the risk of bankruptcy to an inefficiently high level.

Different types of business assets are also taxed at different rates, encouraging firms to invest more heavily in favored assets than they otherwise would. The depreciation allowances that apply to machines and equipment are relatively generous compared to depreciation allowances for structures and capital-recovery methods for inventory, leading to a relatively light tax burden for machines and equipment. Thus, firms' asset choices are distorted, encouraging more investment in machines and equipment and less in structures and inventory than is economically efficient.

Prior to the Tax Reform of Act of 1986, the differential tax burdens among assets were substantial—a consequence of a relatively high statutory tax rate, relatively high inflation, uneven depreciation rules, and the availability of an investment tax credit for equipment, but not other assets. The 1986 act altered depreciation rules, repealed the investment credit, and reduced the statutory corporate tax rate, thereby greatly diminishing inter-asset distortions. In recent years, however, both legislation and economic developments have reintroduced differential tax burdens, though not to the extent existent before 1986. Legislative changes included introduction of less-favorable depreciation for structures, bonus depreciation for equipment, and an increased statutory tax rate.[11]

As noted above, the corporate income tax distorts corporate financial policy, favoring debt finance. Another distortion of corporate financial policy results from individual rather than corporate income taxation, and the preferential treatment of capital gains. Specifically, since capital gains are not subject to individual income taxes until a stockholder sells stock and the gains are realized, taxes favor the corporate retention of earnings—which increases the value of corporate stock—over payout of dividends. Recent legislation has reduced the statutory tax rate on dividends to the same rate applicable to realized capital gains, which has reduced the difference between the effective tax rates of retentions and payouts. Nonetheless, a difference remains because capital gains are not taxed until realized while dividends are taxed on a current basis.

Business Taxes and Equity

Corporations are not people: they are economic entities (firms) taking a particular legal form (incorporation). Thus, corporations cannot bear the burden of the corporate income tax in any real sense: it ultimately is borne by individuals. In the short run—that is, before economic actors have had a chance to adjust to the tax—the tax is thought to be borne by corporate stockholders

The long-run burden of the tax is more uncertain. The standard and most resilient economic model of the corporate income tax is that developed by Arnold Harberger in 1962.[12] While a number of challenges have been made to the model since its inception, its results have generally proved resilient.[13] The model concludes that if capital investment funds and labor are free to flow from one economic sector (e.g., the corporate sector) to another (and given certain other conditions), then wages, prices, rates of return, and the allocation of capital and labor adjust, in the long run, to the corporate income tax. Given the ability of economic actors to adjust, the burden of the corporate income tax spreads beyond corporate shareholders' sector to all owners of capital, including owners of corporate debt, non-corporate business, and owner-occupied housing.

This picture of the long-run burden of the corporate tax has implications for the vertical equity of the tax system—that is, its distribution across income classes. Because capital ownership is greater at upper-income levels, the corporate income tax is itself progressive and makes the overall tax system more progressive than it would otherwise be.

Business Taxes and Competitiveness

A widely cited reason for reforming U.S. business taxation is to improve U.S. "competitiveness," where competitiveness is usually a loosely defined term generally meaning the ability of U.S. firms to compete with foreign businesses, whether by means of export sales or sales by U.S. firms who have invested abroad. Yet there are few areas in which economic theory and popular beliefs diverge more widely than in international economics and notions of "competitiveness." Given the prominence of competitiveness in the public debate, it is thus useful to examine the international dimension of business taxes' effects in some detail.

Taxes and Trade

Contrary to popular arguments that are sometimes made, economic theory indicates that business taxes do not affect the nation's balance of trade—that is, the imposition of federal taxes on business profits does not increase the U.S. trade deficit by reducing U.S. exports or increasing imports. This conclusion may counter intuition at first—surely the imposition of a tax on the profits of a U.S. exporting firm will reduce its sales to foreigners and thus reduce aggregate U.S. exports. But economic theory's rebuttal is equally intuitive: just as an individual cannot consume more than he earns unless he borrows, a country cannot use more than it produces—cannot import more than it exports—unless it borrows to finance the difference by importing foreign investment. Thus, a country can only increase its trade deficit if it imports some additional amount of foreign investment; a country's net exports only increase if its net overseas investment also increases.[14]

In slightly more technical terms, a country's balance of trade (its balance on goods and services) mirrors its balance on capital account; the balance of trade changes only if the balance on capital account likewise changes. This relationship is an identity that holds whether or not the international economy is in equilibrium. The particular economic mechanism that enforces the identity under the current regime of flexible exchange rates is exchange rate adjustments. Even if a change in an exogenous variable (e.g., taxes) would otherwise increase net exports, exchange rates adjust to offset any change that would otherwise occur.

The implication of this analysis is that business taxes alter the balance of trade only if they also alter net flows of international investment (the balance on capital account). As an illustration, the United States repealed a tax benefit for exporting known as the extraterritorial income (ETI) benefit in 2004. Some observers feared that ETI's repeal would harm U.S. competitiveness. Economic theory, however, suggests that ETI's repeal would have no direct impact on the balance of trade. While some reduction of exports may initially occur, that reduction will stimulate a fall in the price of the dollar in currency markets below what would otherwise occur. The dollar's depreciation will mitigate the initial decline in exports and will also reduce imports. There will be no change in the trade balance (exports minus imports).

While business taxes do not affect the trade balance, they can affect the composition of its trade. This outcome follows from one of the foundations of economic trade theory—the theory of comparative advantage. According to this theory, the composition of a country's exports and imports is determined not by how the costs of domestic goods compare to those of foreign goods, but rather by how the costs of domestic goods compare to each other. Under comparative advantage, a country exports what it can produce at lowest cost. The particular composition of its exports and imports thus depends on the particular pattern of costs across all of its products and potential products. Business taxes can alter this pattern of costs and thus alter the content of trade. For example, if taxes apply heavily to one item and fall lightly on another, they encourage the import of the first product and the export of the second.

But if business taxes cannot increase net exports and can only change the pattern of trade, this is not necessarily bad news. Standard economic trade theory indicates that countries gain economic welfare by exchanging exports for imports; the exchange enables each trading country to specialize in producing what it produces most efficiently while not sacrificing its use of the higher-cost goods that it imports. In short, a country's economic welfare is not enhanced by the mere act of exporting; it is the ability to exchange exports for imports that makes a country better off (that produces "gains from trade," in economic parlance).

Taxes can reduce economic welfare through their impact on trade in a number of ways. One is a reduction in economic efficiency similar to those described in preceding section, but translated to the international economy. If taxes apply unevenly, they may distort the pattern of costs within the economy and distort the composition of trade, thus encouraging a country to specialize in activities at which it is relatively inefficient. A second way taxes can reduce a country's economic welfare is to worsen its "terms of trade," or the quantity (in real terms) of exports it must give up to obtain a given quantity of imports. For example, if part of the benefit of an export subsidy (e.g., ETI) is passed on to foreign consumers in the form of lower prices, the subsidy worsens the subsidizing country's terms of trade; its exports are cheaper for foreign consumers. The subsidizing country's economic welfare is reduced because its own taxpayers are underwriting the price reduction for foreign consumers.

Taxes and International Business Investment

Business taxes can have a direct impact on the extent to which U.S. firms invest abroad, and also the extent to which foreign firms invest in the United States. Here, the crucial factor is how taxes (both U.S. and foreign) on an investment in a foreign location compare to taxes on an identical investment undertaken in the United States. To the extent taxes in the foreign location are lower than those on the U.S. project, taxes encourage overseas investment; to the extent U.S. taxes are low relative to taxes on the overseas investment, they encourage domestic, over foreign, investment. If taxes are the same in either location, they have no impact (are "neutral") on location choice.

According to traditional economic theory, taxes best promote economic efficiency by not distorting the location of investment; neutrality between overseas and domestic investment best promotes efficiency. But the overall impact of the U.S. system is uncertain. As described above, the United States in some situations taxes the overseas income of its firms on a current basis, while in other instances it permits an indefinite deferral of taxes on foreign-source income; foreign tax credits are provided to alleviate double taxation. The net result of this system for the relative tax burden on foreign and domestic investment is mixed; the system produces a patchwork of incentives, disincentives, and neutrality towards overseas investment that varies, depending on factors such as the level of foreign taxes applied to the investment, the legal form of the investment, and the location and nature of a firm's other foreign investments. The efficiency effect of the system is thus not clear.

Business Taxes and Tax Reform

The first section of this report outlined the current structure of federal business taxation—a separate tax on corporate profits imposed in addition to the individual income tax and net of interest; and taxation of unincorporated business on a current basis under the individual income tax. The report's section on business tax data indicated that while the level of business taxes has generally declined since World War II, important divergences remain in the way different types of investment are taxed. The section on economic effects indicated that these effects can impair economic efficiency, although they likely do not hinder U.S. competitiveness. With these pictures in mind, the report now turns to the principal options for reform that have been developed for business tax policy.

Comprehensive Taxation of Business Income

Since corporations are economic and legal entities and not people, the question might be raised: why impose a separate corporate income tax at all?

The question is made more pointed when the detrimental efficiency effects of a separate tax on corporate income are considered—effects such as the diversion of investment away from equity investment in the corporate sector. A number of arguments, however, can be mounted in favor of a separate tax on corporate income. First, since stock ownership in particular, and ownership of capital in general, is more prevalent among upper-income individuals, the corporate income tax adds an element of progressivity to the tax system; its repeal—absent compensating changes elsewhere in the system—would be, in isolation, a regressive policy change. Second, corporate managers may be able to exercise considerable independence from stockholders in their decisions about corporate investment. To the extent this occurs, corporations do have some existence separate from their stockholders. Third, without a corporate income tax (or tax integration plan, as outlined below), retained corporate earnings would receive favorable tax treatment. And finally, even if corporations are not people and have no existence separate from their stockholders, many individual taxpayers nonetheless compare the taxes they pay with those paid by large corporations and draw conclusions about fairness from that comparison. And even if such comparisons, from an economic standpoint, are not appropriate, they do affect perceptions about the fairness of the tax system—perceptions that are important to the acceptance of the tax system by the public at large.

While the current system does tax corporations as though they were separate entities, it does not do so on a comprehensive basis. Numerous important omissions from the tax base would exist if all corporate profits were taxed on the same basis. Thus, if the validity of a separate corporate income tax is accepted, one hypothetical direction that tax reform might take is to move in the direction of a more pure version of the "classical" system of taxing corporate income—to eliminate the various omissions in the tax base and non-neutralities embedded in the current system. Setting aside the distortions that result from the existence of the corporate income tax in the first place, such a reform would likely minimize the inefficiencies and distortions that exist within the classical system. As noted at the outset of the report, such was a guiding principle of the Tax Reform Act of 1986.

How much does the current system depart from a comprehensive tax on corporate income? One considerable departure is the omission of income from debt-financed investment from the tax base—an omission that occurs when interest payments are deducted. Income generated by debt-financed investment is income from capital just as surely as is income from equity investment. Debt's omission from the tax base distorts firms' financing choices, favoring debt over equity and enticing firms to accept a higher risk of bankruptcy than is economically efficient. Nonetheless, simple elimination of interest deductibility has rarely been proposed outside of a movement away from the classical system by adoption, for example, of tax integration (discussed below).[15]

Another important determinant of the corporate tax base is depreciation. One important element of the 1986 act's reform was its evening-out of depreciation allowances across assets. The act implemented depreciation allowances that were more closely aligned with actual economic depreciation. Together with the act's repeal of the investment tax credit, the depreciation revisions reduced prior law's general preference for equipment and relatively short-lived assets over structures. Since 1986, however, a wedge has reemerged between equipment and structures, although—setting aside the temporary bonus depreciation for equipment—this has been more a consequence of changed economic conditions (reduced inflation) and a lengthening of depreciation allowances for structures than reintroduction of accelerated depreciation.[16] Nonetheless, a likely ingredient of tax reform based on comprehensive income taxation would be a realignment of depreciation allowances with economic depreciation.

Another prominent departure from comprehensive taxation is the deduction for domestic production that was enacted by the American Jobs Creation Act of 2004 (P.L. 108-357). The deduction is 9% of income from domestic production activities; it cannot be applied to income from overseas investment. Other omissions from the tax base are more narrowly targeted tax benefits—for example, the section 179 expensing allowance from equipment investment of small businesses, the tax credit for research and experimentation, and various provisions applicable to the oil and gas industry. The Joint Committee on Taxation (JCT) maintains a list of "tax expenditures" or provisions that carve out special tax treatment for particular activities, income, or investments; a relatively comprehensive list of omissions from the corporate tax base can be obtained by consulting the JCT list.[17] A tax reform that moves in the direction of comprehensive income taxation would presumably scale back items included in the list of tax expenditures.

Corporate Tax Integration

As described above in the section on the economic effects of business taxation, the current "classical" system of taxing corporate income results in a number of distortions in the allocation of investment, thus reducing economic efficiency and causing a concomitant reduction in economic welfare. For this reason, economists have long advocated some form of tax "integration"—a term that refers to eliminating double taxation of corporate income by altering the general system of taxing corporate-source income.

Integration proposals vary, but fall into two broad categories: those that apply to both retained earnings and dividends and thus all corporate profits ("full integration"), and those that change the treatment only of earnings that are distributed ("partial integration").

There are three basic approaches to full integration, which differ in whether double taxation is removed at the corporate level or at the individual level. The "shareholder allocation" method is similar to partnership taxation. The corporate income tax would be repealed, and corporate profits—whether retained or distributed—would be allocated among the firm's owners, who would pay individual income taxes on the corporate income. Thus, corporate income would be taxed once, in the hands of individuals.

A second approach is "shareholder credit" integration, under which the corporate income tax would be retained, but corporate stockholders would receive a tax credit for the corporate-level taxes paid by the paying corporation. An adjustment to the capital gains portion of the credit would be made to account for the capital gains resulting from both retained earnings (that have been subject to the corporate income tax) and other price appreciation. Under this approach, while relief would be provided at the individual level, taxes would be paid on the corporate income tax at individual income tax rates. Thus, the corporate income tax would function much like a withholding tax.

A third approach is to retain the corporate income tax, but exclude corporate-source income from individual income taxes—a relatively simple method to implement for distributed earnings, but difficult to administer for the portion of capital gains attributable to reinvested earnings. In the latter case, stockholders' basis in stock would have to be adjusted to reflect retained earnings, so as to exclude only gains attributable to retained earnings. In 1992, a U.S. Treasury report outlined a variant of this method, termed a "comprehensive business income tax" (CBIT), under which corporate-source income would not be taxed at the individual level. The corporate income tax would be retained, and interest deductions would not be permitted.

Partial integration by means of an exclusion for dividends received by stockholders would thus be relatively straightforward. Indeed, the reduced individual income tax rate that the Jobs and Growth Tax Relief Act of 2003

(JGTRRA) applied to dividend income can be viewed as a form of shareholder-level partial integration, akin to a shareholder exclusion that applies to only part of received dividends. Similarly, a shareholder-credit version of integration that would be restricted to dividends paid would be more straightforward than the full-integration version of a credit system. A partial-integration form of the shareholder credit method is the system used most frequently by European and other foreign countries that have adopted integration.

Each method of integration has its particular advantages and disadvantages. As suggested in the preceding discussion, partial integration is simpler and easier to administer than full integration; on the other hand, it does not achieve all the efficiency gains under full integration, since a part of corporate income would still be taxed twice. Also, the different plans differ in their revenue cost, with the full-integration methods generally losing more revenue than partial integration plans, and shareholder allocation methods reducing revenue more than other methods.[18]

Business Taxes under Consumption or Flat Taxes

Either tax integration or a tax based on a comprehensive measure of income would qualify as fundamental tax reform. Each would entail substantial changes to the current system and would use a tax base supported by a relatively consistent concept of income. In popular discussions, however, the term "fundamental tax reform" has frequently referred to a different type of tax change: replacing the current federal individual and corporate income taxes with a system that taxes consumption but exempts saving. Most taxonomies list three basic types of national-level consumption taxes: value-added taxes; a national sales tax; and a tax on individuals' consumed income. In addition, a prominent "flat tax" proposal would consist of a form of value-added tax imposed at the corporate level and a wage tax at the individual level.

The different forms of consumption taxes differ chiefly in their methods of collection and, as a result, their ease of administration and compliance costs. Their general effect on business taxes, however, would be the same: income from new business investment would be exempt from tax under each form. In the near term, however, income from investment in place at the time of transition would generally be taxed.

National Sales Tax

Turning to specifics, a national retail sales tax would operate much as do the sales taxes imposed by most states: the tax would be imposed on final sales from businesses to consumers; businesses would collect the tax and remit it to the government. In general, business-to-business sales (sales of intermediate goods) would be exempt from the tax; the levy would be applied to imports, but exported goods would be exempt.

To the extent that business inputs are included in the base of a national sales tax, the product to which they contribute would be subject to multiple layers of tax; such cascading would carry the potential of inefficient distortions, diverting resources away from the heavily taxed products. Accordingly, an important task under a national sales tax would be distinguishing between business and non-business uses of purchased items, so as to exempt the former and tax the latter. One possible method of doing so would be to issue exemption certificates to businesses so as to remove their purchases from the tax base. Nonetheless, making the distinction would likely present significant administrative and compliance problems, particularly in the case of items that lend themselves to both business and personal use (e.g., many services). Compliance might also present a problem, given the high tax rate that would likely be necessary to avoid a revenue loss if income taxes were abolished.[19]

Value-Added Tax and "Flat" Tax

As the term implies, value-added taxes (VAT) are levied on the value added by each firm in a good's production process. VATs thus differ in their point of collection from retail sales taxes, but by the final stage of production the cumulative rate of the VAT on an item is the same as that of a sales tax (assuming each is applied uniformly).

There are two general methods by which VATs are administered: credit-invoice and subtraction. Under a credit-invoice method, a business is assessed VAT on its gross receipts, regardless of whether its sales are made to another business or to a final consumer. At the same time, the firms from which it has purchased its inputs provide it with invoices showing the VAT the suppliers have already paid with respect to the inputs. The purchasing firm claims the VAT shown on the invoice as a credit against the VAT on its own sales. As a result, for each firm, the VAT applies only to value added. Under a subtraction-method VAT, tax is levied on a firm's gross receipts after subtracting purchases from other firms. What is left, then, as the base of the tax is the return to capital (profits) and the return to labor (wages)—the value added by the taxed firm. Despite the difference in administration, a subtraction-method VAT and a credit-invoice VAT produce the same tax, assuming they are levied at the same rate. It should also be noted that, as with a sales tax, each is levied on imports, but exports are not included in taxable gross receipts. In the case of the credit-invoice method, an exporting firm receives a tax rebate for taxes paid with respect to its inputs.

A variation on the subtraction-method VAT is the so-called "flat tax"—sometimes termed the Hall-Rabushka proposal after its designers. Under the flat tax, a subtraction-method VAT would be imposed on business—that is, firms would pay a tax on gross receipts minus items purchased from other firms. In contrast to a pure VAT, however, firms would also be permitted to subtract wages from gross income, thus removing from the business-level tax base that portion of the firm's value-added contributed by labor. Individuals, however, would be assessed a tax on wages received, thus bringing the value added by labor back into the tax base, albeit at the individual level.

By the final stage of production, the cumulative rate of a VAT on an item is the same as that of a sales tax, assuming neither contains special allowances and benefits. Thus, their broad economic effects are the same. But since the two types of tax differ in how they are collected, there are differences in compliance and ease of administration. A VAT would impose a higher compliance burden on businesses in general than a retail sales tax; under a VAT, every business would be required to file a tax return, not just businesses in the retail sector. At the same time, a VAT avoids the administrative problem of distinguishing business use of items from personal use. Further, some analysts have argued that small businesses would likely encounter high compliance costs under a national sales tax, and small businesses are relatively numerous in the retail sector. Thus, compliance rates may be higher under a VAT.

Consumed Income Tax

A third type of consumption tax is a tax on consumed income imposed at the individual rather than business level. Individual income consists of consumption plus saving. Thus, individuals would calculate their tax by subtracting saving from their income and paying tax on the residual. Business investments made by individuals would be characterized as saving, and thus an exempt use of income. Thus, for example, an individual's purchases of stock would be deducted from taxable income, as would, say, the purchase of a new machine by a small business owner. Note that an individual consumption tax is defined in terms of the uses of income rather than its source. Thus, it is business investment that is deductible rather than income generated by businesses. However, arithmetic dictates that deducting the cost of a capital investment at the time it is made ("expensing" the investment) produces a tax saving that is identical in present-value terms to exempting the net income the investment produces as it is generated over the investment's lifetime. Thus, deducting business investment on the uses side of the income ledger is the same as exempting income from new investment on the sources side. New business investment bears no burden under an individual consumption tax.

Effects of a Consumption Tax on Business

A consumption tax exempts from its coverage income that is saved, which is the equivalent of exempting investment income. In short, under any form of pure consumption tax—be it a sales tax, a VAT, or an individual consumption tax—business profits are ultimately exempt from tax. As a result, if it is assumed that a consumption tax would not contain its own preferences for special goods or services (an assumption that is perhaps heroic), the various non-neutralities existing under the current system of business taxation would be eliminated. As described in the preceding section on economic efficiency, these include current law's preference of non-corporate investment over the corporate sector, of corporate debt over equity, and of machines and equipment over inventory and structures. If these non-neutralities were eliminated under a consumption tax, business investment—especially corporate investment—could be expected to increase under a consumption tax, as well as equity finance and investment in assets other than equipment. Economic efficiency could potentially increase.

It is worth underlining, however, that it is not the taxation of capital per se that produces these non-neutralities, but the particular shape of capital income taxation that has gradually come into being in the current system. Under a consumption tax, non-neutralities affecting business might be implemented in a different way, but the result might still be distortions in the allocation in business investment. For example, a sales tax or VAT might exempt a particular type of good from taxation, which would favor investment in the sector producing that type of good.

The transition to a consumption tax would likely include significant effects in the short and medium term. Perhaps most importantly, a consumption tax would exempt the return to new investment, but would still apply to income produced by investment in place at the time of the tax's implementation. Note that under none of the types of consumption taxes outlined above would a firm be able to continue to recover the cost of capital in place at the time of transition, either through depreciation or other deductions. At the same time, revenue produced by old investments would be included in the tax base, producing a windfall loss for owners of existing capital. Firms affected most heavily by the taxation of old capital would be older, slow-growing firms. Also, if a uniform consumption tax were adopted and existing business distortions were consequently eliminated, as described above, transition effects would include a shift of resources away from previously favored investment. For example, business sectors where corporate production is intensive would benefit, as would firms with low debt-to-equity ratios and production processes favoring machines and equipment over structures.[20]

A frequently made popular argument for a consumption tax relates to its purported beneficial effects on competitiveness. As described above under the heading "Taxes and Trade," economic theory indicates taxes have little impact on competitiveness as it is popularly understood. However, a specific argument relating to "border tax adjustments" is frequently made in support of consumption taxes, so the argument is worth describing here. The argument—frequently made by businesses—focuses on the fact that foreign firms in VAT countries receive a rebate of the VAT on exports to the United States and elsewhere. Thus, it is argued, foreign firms from VAT countries have a cost advantage over competing U.S. firms. As described in the section on competitiveness, however, taxes or tax-related mechanisms such as VAT rebates do not directly alter the balance of trade. In the particular case of VAT rebates, exchange rate adjustments in response to the rebates act to eliminate any impact on the balance of trade or "competitiveness."

CONCLUSION

While the charts presented earlier in this report show that the level of the corporate tax has generally fallen in the decades since World War II, the basic structure has remained the same: a "classical" system under which the corporate income tax is superimposed on the individual income tax. In 1986, the far-reaching Tax Reform Act implemented reforms within the context of the existing system, broadening its base and reducing rates. In recent years, however, concern about the impact of the system on capital formation and U.S. performance in international markets has stimulated interest in a more substantial structural change, either by adopting tax integration or moving towards a consumption tax.

End Notes

[1] Bonus depreciation was initially provided by the Job Creation and Worker Assistance Act of 2002 (JCWA; P.L. 107- 147). It was increased by the Jobs and Growth Tax Relief and Reconciliation Act of 2003 (JGTRRA; P.L. 108-27) but generally does not apply to property placed in service after 2004. The domestic production deduction was provided by the American Job Creation Act of 2004 (AJCA; P.L. 108-357).

[2] For a more detailed description of the taxation of passthrough entities, see CRS Report RL31538, *Passthrough Organizations Not Taxed As Corporations*, by Jack H. Taylor (out of print, available from the author). See also CRS Report RL32254, *Small Business Tax Benefits: Overview and Economic Rationale*, by Gary Guenther.

[3] U.S. Congressional Budget Office, *Taxing Capital Income: Effective Rates and Approaches to Reform* (Washington: GPO, 2005), p. 19.

[4] An exception is income earned by corporations subject to the alternative minimum tax (AMT). AMT rules in some cases apply differently to corporations compared to individuals.

[5] More precisely, METRs begin by assuming that investments must earn a particular return, after taxes, in order to attract funds from savers. The METR calculation then works backwards, and derives a pre-tax return investments must earn in order to generate the after-tax return required by savers. The difference between the pre-tax and after-tax returns is sometimes referred to as the "tax wedge." An investment's METR consists of the tax wedge divided by the pre-tax return.

[6] For a discussion of factors underlying the variation in METRs, see CRS Report RS21706, *Historical Effective Marginal Tax Rates on Capital Income*, by Jane G. Gravelle.

[7] Tax distortions among assets also persist within the corporate sector. While differential treatment of assets declined under the Tax Reform Act of 1986, subsequent changes in law have reintroduced significant differences in the treatment of equipment, structures, and inventories, with equipment being favored. See CRS Report RL32099, *Capital Income Tax Revisions and Effective Tax Rates*, by Jane G. Gravelle. See also U.S. Congressional Budget Office, *Taxing Capital Income: Effective Rates and Approaches to Reform* (Washington: GPO, 2005), p. 8.

[8] Some economists have concluded that the distortions from taxing capital are so great that the optimal tax on capital from the point of view of economic efficiency and welfare is zero. Acceptance of this analysis, even in principle, requires a particular theoretical construct that includes, for example, an assumption that individuals have infinitely lived time horizons. But even if this analysis is accepted, it does not necessarily recommend a repeal of capital

income taxation for a number of reasons: the unresponsiveness of saving may reduce any distortions; any tax that replaces a tax on capital likely has its own distortions; and the transition costs of moving to an alternative tax may be costly enough to offset any benefit.

[9] For a thorough survey of the empirical studies that have been conducted, see B. Douglas Bernheim, "Taxation and Saving," *Handbook of Public Economics*, vol. 3, Alan J. Auerbach and Martin Feldstein, eds., (Amsterdam: Elsevier, 2002), pp. 1173-1249. Note also that while investment incentives may not result in additional domestic saving, they may attract foreign capital into the domestic economy. The return to foreign capital, however, does not accrue to domestic residents.

[10] For a textbook presentation of this argument, see Andrew B. Abel and Ben S. Bernanke, *Macroeconomics*, 3rd ed. (Reading, MA: Addison-Wesley, 1998), p. 210.

[11] Jane G. Gravelle, "The Corporate Tax: Where Has it Been and Where is it Going?" *National Tax Journal*, vol. 57, Dec. 2004, p. 914.

[12] Arnold H. Harberger, "The Incidence of the Corporation Income Tax," *Journal of Political Economy,* vol. 70, June 1962, pp. 215-240.

[13] See the review of challenges to the Harberger model in Jane G. Gravelle, "The Corporate Income Tax: Economic Issues and Policy Options," *National Tax Journal*, vol. 48, June, 1995, pp. 267-277.

[14] Note, however, that a country's general fiscal position can alter the trade balance. For example, if a country increases its government's budget deficit, real interest rates may rise, leading to an inflow of foreign capital and an expansion of its trade deficit. Thus, to the extent business taxes contribute to total government revenue and the government's overall fiscal stance, they can be said to have an impact on the trade deficit. In this sense, however, they are indistinguishable from other taxes.

[15] For example, even the initial, more theoretically pure, Treasury Department proposals that preceded the 1986 Tax Reform Act stopped short of straightforward taxation of the return to debt.

[16] For estimates of disparities in tax burdens across assets under current law, see CRS Report RL32099, *Capital Income Tax Revisions and Effective Tax Rates*, by Jane G. Gravelle.

[17] CRS has prepared for the Senate Budget Committee a compendium containing explanations and analyses of the various tax expenditures on a biannual basis. The most recent version is U.S. Congress, Senate Committee on the Budget, *Tax Expenditures: Compendium of Background Material on Individual Provisions*, 110th Cong., 2nd sess., December 2008, S. Prt. 110-667 (Washington: GPO, 2008).

[18] For a more comprehensive discussion and analysis of integration, see CRS Report RL31597, *The Taxation of ividend Income: An Overview and Economic Analysis of the Issues*, by Jane G. Gravelle.

[19] For more detailed discussions of how a national sales tax might operate in practice, see John L. Mikesell, "The American Retail Sales Tax: Considerations on Their Structure, Operations, and Potential as a Foundation for a Federal Sales Tax," *National Tax Journal*, vol. 50, Mar. 1997, pp. 149-165, and Martin Sullivan, *Flat Taxes and Consumption Taxes: A Guide to the Debate* (Washington: American Institute of Certified Public Accountants, 1995), pp. 11-18.

[20] For a more detailed analysis of the impact of fundamental tax reform on business, see CRS Report RL32603, *The Flat Tax, Value-Added Tax, and National Retail Sales Tax: Overview of the Issues*, by Jane G. Gravelle.

In: Business Taxation
Editors: J. C. Teague and K. Fawner
ISBN: 978-1-62257-998-3

Chapter 3

TAXING LARGE PASS-THROUGHS AS CORPORATIONS: HOW MANY FIRMS WOULD BE AFFECTED?*

Mark P. Keightley

SUMMARY

Several lawmakers and the Obama Administration have expressed interest in taxing large partnerships and S corporations, also known as pass-throughs, as corporations. Part of this interest appears to be related to deficit and debt concerns. Pass-throughs may be a source of revenue since they currently account for over half of all business income but generally pay no corporate tax. Additionally, there is a growing concern that the current business tax environment may be inequitable and inefficient. Today, two business that are otherwise identical except that one is a corporation and the other is a pass-through are taxed differently. This disparity could be viewed as inequitable since the companies are similarly positioned to pay taxes.

Additionally, the lack of tax uniformity across business types may cause an inefficient allocation of resources if business decisions are made for tax reasons and not economic reasons. This report uses aggregate and industry-level tax data to analyze how many partnerships and S

* This is an edited, reformatted and augmented version of a Congressional Research Service publication, CRS Report for Congress R42451, from www.crs.gov, prepared for Members and Committees of Congress, dated March 30, 2012.

corporations could be subject to the corporate tax. It is estimated that if a receipt-based measure of size is used, then between 0.3% and 1.5% of S corporations and partnerships could be taxed as corporations depending on if a "large" pass-through is defined as one with receipts exceeding $50 million or exceeding $10 million. Using an asset-based measure of size produces similar estimates. It is estimated that between 0.3% and 1.0% of pass-throughs could pay the corporate tax depending on whether a $100 million or $25 million asset threshold is used to define a "large" firm.

Although estimates suggest that only a small percentage of pass-throughs could be considered large for corporate tax purposes, this report also finds that those firms are responsible for a significant amount of economic activity, indicating that the proposed policy change could raise substantial revenue. For example, 30% of S corporation receipts are generated by the largest 0.3% of S corporations, and 41% of partnership receipts are generated by the largest 0.2% of partnerships. Similarly, the largest 0.2% of S corporations hold 43% of S corporation assets, while the largest 1.1% of partnerships hold 78% of partnership assets.

Taxing large pass-throughs as corporations would also allow for lower tax rates as it would broaden the corporate tax base. Lower tax rates combined with a reduction in the tax disparity between the corporate and non-corporate sectors could improve business tax equity and the allocation of resources relative to current policy. At the same time, an alternative policy prescription that is generally more appealing to economists—integration of the corporate and individual tax systems—could also achieve these objectives. If integration is not possible, however, then reducing the tax discrepancy between large pass-throughs and corporations may be another viable alternative, depending on its design.

INTRODUCTION

Several lawmakers and the Obama Administration have recently expressed interest in taxing large partnerships and S corporations, also known as pass-throughs, as corporations. In early 2011, Senate Finance Committee Chairman Max Baucus suggested the possibility of taxing pass-throughs earning above a certain income as corporations.[1] That same year, Treasury Secretary Tim Geithner said "Congress has to revisit this basic question about whether it makes sense for us as a country to allow certain businesses to choose whether they're treated as corporations for tax purposes or not."[2] Most recently the President proposed creating parity in the tax treatment of large corporate and non-corporate businesses.[3] House Ways and Means Committee

Chairman Dave Camp, however, has expressed his opposition to such a policy change.[4]

Two concerns appear to be driving the interest in taxing large pass-throughs as corporations. First, projected deficit and debt increases have highlighted the possible need for revenue increases. Pass-throughs may be a source of revenue since they currently comprise over half of all business income but generally pay no corporate tax.[5] Instead, the income of these companies, as the name suggests, "passes through" the business directly to the owners where it is taxed according to individual tax rates.[6] Although no official revenue estimates exist, calculations by economist Martin Sullivan suggest that federal tax revenues may be between $13 billion and $47 billion lower annually than could otherwise be expected because of the shift away from the corporate form towards the pass-through forms.[7] The shift has led to a reduction in corporate tax revenues, which has not been completely offset by increased individual tax revenue.

Second, discussions of tax reform have expressed concern about the equity, efficiency, and complexity of the general business tax environment in existence today, and in some cases the distinction between corporate and non-corporate businesses specifically.[8] Today, two businesses that are otherwise identical other than that one is a corporation and one is a pass-through are taxed differently. This disparity could be viewed as inequitable since the firms are similarly positioned to pay taxes. Additionally, the lack of tax uniformity across business types is believed to result in too much investment in the non-corporate sector where the after-tax return on investment is higher.[9] Taxing large pass-throughs as corporations, when combined with other reform proposals such as eliminating or reducing corporate tax preferences and loopholes, would broaden the corporate tax base and allow for lower tax rates. These changes could potentially increase economic efficiency relative to the current policy. Estimates by CRS suggest that limiting the ability to avoid corporate taxation could potentially broaden the base enough to allow for a revenue-neutral corporate rate reduction of three percentage points.[10]

This report uses aggregate and industry-level tax data to analyze how many partnerships and S corporations could be subject to the corporate tax. Analysis of the data suggests that between 0.3% and 1.5% of all partnerships and S corporations could be taxed as corporations depending on what constitutes a "large" pass-through. Although this fraction is a relatively small share of pass-throughs, this report also indicates that these largest pass-throughs account for a disproportionate share of receipts and assets. Thus, while only a small number of firms may be affected by such a proposed policy change, the revenue generated could potentially be significant.

There are alternative policy prescriptions that can promote business tax uniformity and increase efficiency. Integrating the corporate and individual tax systems so that all business income is only taxed once is one such alternative. Integration would promote tax uniformity since all businesses would be taxed equally. Integration could also increase efficiency by removing a layer of taxation as well as possibly other distorting features of the corporate tax. For these reasons integration is generally appealing to economists. If, for whatever reason, integration is not possible, then reducing the tax discrepancy between large pass-throughs and corporations may be a viable policy alternative. The various design and administrative issues surrounding tax integration, however, put an analysis of such a proposal beyond the scope of this report.[11]

The impact on businesses is not the only perspective one can take when it comes to changing the tax treatment of pass-throughs. CRS Report *Who Earns Pass-Through Business Income? An Analysis of Individual Tax Return Data*, by Mark P. Keightley examined the issue of pass-through taxation from the perspective of individual taxpayers. That report concluded that although the corporate tax would be levied on pass-throughs, individuals would bear the full burden of the tax since businesses are legal, not physical entities. In addition, the analysis in that report suggests that higher-income taxpayers would generally bear most of the burden from increased pass-through taxes because they earn the majority of pass-through income and are limited in their ability to shift the burden to lower-income taxpayers.

The remainder of this report is organized as follows. First, a brief overview of tax revenue and trends in business organization is presented. Next, pass-throughs are compared with their corporate counterparts. Aggregate and industry-level estimates of the number of partnerships and S corporations that could be taxed as corporations are then presented. Finally, policy options and considerations are reviewed.

TRENDS IN TAX REVENUE AND BUSINESS ORGANIZATION

Part of the interest in taxing large pass-throughs as corporations stems from the decline in corporate tax revenue. In the post-World War II era, corporate tax revenue as a share of gross domestic product (GDP) peaked in 1952 at 6.1% and has generally declined since (see *Figure 1*). Today, the corporate tax generates revenue equal to approximately 1.3% of GDP, although projections (not shown here) have the corporate tax revenue rising to 2.4% of GDP in several years as the economy recovers and temporary investment incentives (bonus depreciation) expire. Despite this decline, an increase in payroll tax revenue from 1.4% of GDP in 1946 to 6.0% in 2010 has helped to support overall federal tax revenue.

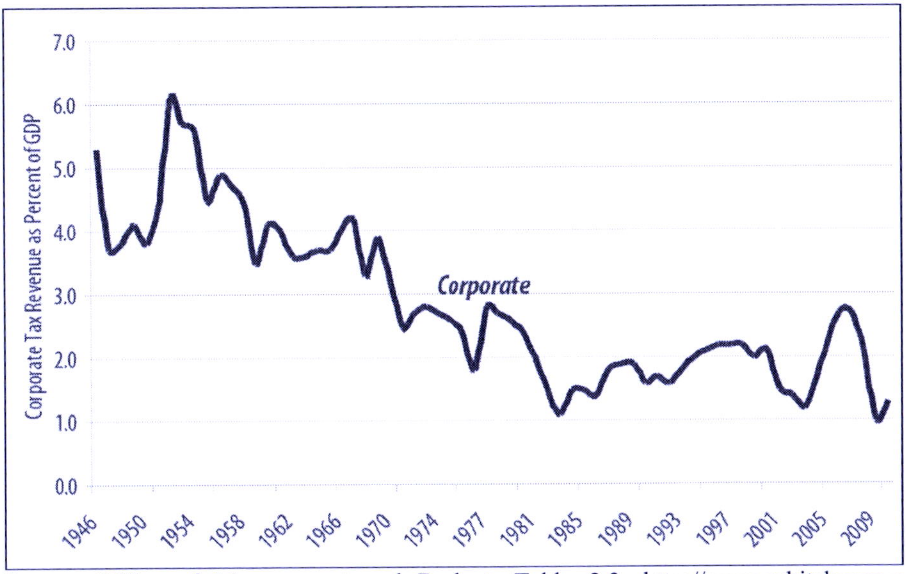

Source: Office of Management and Budget, Table 2.3, http://www.whitehouse.gov/omb/budget/Historicals.

Figure 1. Corporate Tax Revenue As a Percentage of GDP, 1946-2010.

A number of reasons for the decline in corporate tax revenues have been indentified. First, the average effective corporate tax rate has decreased over time, mostly as a result of reductions in the statutory rate and changes affecting the tax treatment of investment and capital recovery (depreciation). Second, corporate-sector profitability has fallen over time, which has eroded the corporate tax base. And third, an increasing fraction of business activity has shifted to partnerships and S corporations, which are not subject to the corporate income tax, further eroding the corporate tax base.

Figure 2 shows just how significant the shift in business activity has been. In 1980, C corporations generated 78% of net business income in the United States. By 2008 however, the corporate sector was responsible for only 27% of all business income. Over the same time period, the share of income attributable to partnerships and S corporations grew from 4% to 54%.[12]

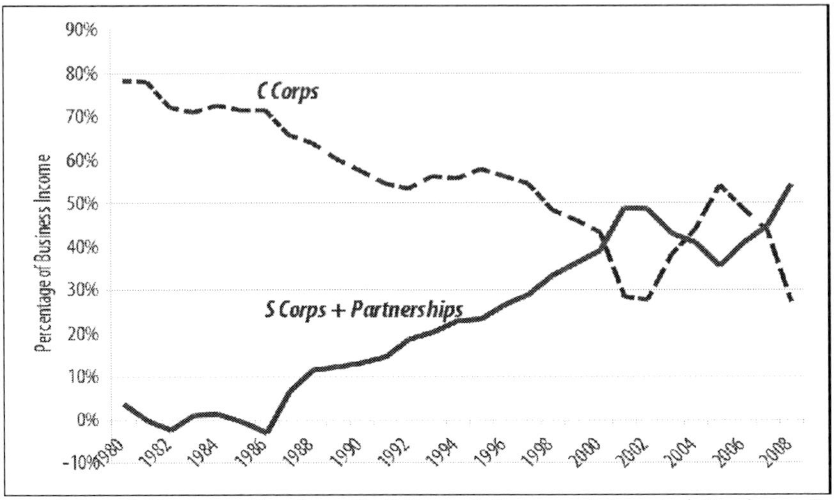

Source: Internal Revenue Service, Statistics of Income, Integrated Business Data, http://www.irs.gov/pub/irs-soi/ 80ot1all.xls.

Notes: Data excludes regulated investment companies (RICs) and Real Estate Investment Trusts (REITs). Sole proprietorships were included in computing aggregate net business income for purposes of determine the distribution shown. Sole proprietorships, however, are overwhelmingly small business and would not likely be subject to the corporate tax. Thus, they are excluded from the figure.

Figure 2. Net Business Income By Business Type, 1980-2008.

These trends are partly due to the Tax Reform Act of 1986 (TRA86), which increased the attractiveness of choosing a pass-through form over the corporate form by lowering the highest individual income tax rate six percentage points below the highest corporate income tax rate.13 Additional legislative changes in the early 1990s allowed S corporations to have more shareholders, and that same decade regulatory changes enabled LLCs to be taxed as partnerships. These policy changes increased the attractiveness of pass-throughs and, in the case of the S corporation shareholder limit increase, allowed them to be larger.

Comparing Large Pass-Throughs and Corporations

How do large pass-throughs compare with corporations? This question is slightly more complicated than it appears since there are several different ways to measure firm size. Size could be measured by employment, profits, assets, or a variety of other statistics. Additionally, two different industries may require different measures of size. For example, one industry may be more capital intensive than another, leading firms in that industry to naturally have more assets, whereas firms in another industry may generally have fewer assets while still employing a large number of workers. Data availability, however, limits the analysis presented here to using just two different measures of firm size—a receipt-based measure and an asset-based measure.

Size Based on Receipts

Table 1 compares large S corporations and partnerships with large corporations based on business receipts. The table displays data for two different categories of firm size—firms with receipts between $10 million and $50 million, and firms with receipts over $50 million. The $10 million to $50 million category arguably contains some firms that many would not consider large since $10 million in receipts is right on the boundary between the definition of a small and medium size business. However, refinement of the size thresholds is impossible since the IRS has already organized the data in this fashion. Still, the category contains some larger pass-throughs since it includes firms with receipts up to $50 million. Without knowing exactly where the receipt threshold may be for the tax it is useful to compare business across both size categories.

Table 1 shows that there were more pass-throughs (87,674) than corporations (67,144) with receipts above $10 million. There were also nearly as many pass-throughs (15,360) as corporations (16,516) with receipts exceeding $50 million. These figures are not too surprising since there are more S corporations and partnerships than C corporations in total. These figures do, however, highlight an important fact that is often overlooked—the term pass-through is not necessarily synonymous with the term "small business."

The data also show that average receipts of medium to large size pass-throughs (firms with receipts of $10 million to $50 million) are nearly identical to average receipts of similar sized corporations. This makes sense given that Table 1 groups the data according to receipts. There is, however, a noticeable difference in the average receipts of the largest pass-throughs and corporations. For corporations with receipts over $50 million, average receipts are nearly $700 million, while the largest S corporations average receipts of

$128 million, and the largest partnerships average receipts of $302 million. Thus, while there are a significant number of large pass-throughs, the largest corporations, when measured by receipts, are over five times larger than the average S corporation, and more than twice as large as the average partnership.

Table 1. Comparison of Large Pass-Throughs and Corporations Based on Business Receipts, 2003 (money amounts are measured in thousands of dollars)

	$10 million under $50 million	*Over $50 million*
C corporations:		
Number of firms	50,628	16,516
Average business receipts	$18,413	$711,304
% of all C corporations	2.5%	0.8%
% of total C corporation receipts	7%	83%
S corporations:		
Number of firms	52,898	9,757
Average business receipts	$20,739	$128,387
% of all S corporations	1.6%	0.3%
% of total S corporation receipts	26%	30%
Partnerships:		
Number of firms	19,416	5,603
Average business receipts	$18,159	$302,106
% of all partnerships	0.8%	0.2%
% of total partnership receipts	8%	41%

Source: CRS calculations using Internal Revenue Service's 2003 Statistics of Income (SOI) Integrated Business Database (IBD), table 2, http://www.irs.gov/pub/irs-soi/03ot2busbr.xls.

Note: The most recent data available that contain information on firm size measured by receipts for all three business types are from 2003.

Another similarity between pass-throughs and corporations is the concentration of receipts among a very small percentage of large firms. About 30% of S corporation receipts are generated by the largest 0.3% of S corporations, and 41% of partnership receipts are generated by the largest 0.2% of partnerships. In comparison, the largest 0.8% of corporations are responsible for 83% of corporate receipts, indicating that there is an even greater concentration of receipts among the largest corporations than there is among the largest pass-throughs. Including firms with receipts between $10 million and $50 million increases the fraction of activity concentrated among large pass-throughs and corporations. Thus, while only a small percentage of partnerships and S corporations could be considered large and therefore subject to the corporate tax, these large passthroughs could potentially generate a significant amount of tax revenue because they account for a disproportionate share of pass-through business activity.

Size Based on Assets

The similarities between large pass-throughs and large corporations extend to a comparison based on total assets. *Table 2* shows that there are at least as many S corporations and partnerships (combined) as C corporations in each of the three size categories.

Table 2. Comparison of Large Pass-Throughs and Corporations Based on Assets, 2008 (money amounts are measured in thousands of dollars)

	$25 million under $50 million	$50 million under $100 million	Over $100 million
C corporations:			
Number of returns	9,377	7,288	20,519
Average assets	$35,486	$71,419	$3,483,793
% of C corporations	0.5%	0.4%	1.1%
% of C corporation assets	1%	1%	97%
S corporations:			
Number of returns	7,551	3,611	3,326
Average assets	$34,471	$69,424	$361,250
% of S corporations	0.2%	0.1%	0.1%
% of S corporation assets	8%	7%	36%
Partnerships:			
Number of returns	25,072	14,272	18,180
Average assets	$34,811	$69,711	$773,236
% of Partnerships	0.8%	0.5%	0.6%
% of Partnership assets	5%	5%	73%

Source: CRS calculations using Internal Revenue Service's SOI, Table Wizard, http://www.taxstatstablewizard.com, and Statistics of Income Tax Stats, Partnership Statistics, http://www.irs.gov/ taxstats/bustaxstats/article/0,,id=97153,00.html.

In 2008, there were 39,389 pass-throughs with assets above $50 million, compared with 27,807 corporations; there were 21,056 pass-throughs with assets exceeding $100 million, compared with 20,519 corporations of the same size. As in the case of a receipt-based comparison, these figures run contrary to the general association of pass-throughs with "small business."

An asset-based comparison also shows that the largest corporations are, again, much larger than the largest pass-throughs. For corporations with assets over $100 million, average assets equal nearly $3.5 billion, while the largest S corporations average assets of $361 million, and the largest partnerships average assets of $773 million. Although there are a significant number of large pass-throughs, the largest corporations are about 4.5 times larger than the average S corporation, and about 10 times larger than the average partnership. This difference between the largest corporations and pass-throughs may be partly due to corporations' access to larger capital markets with which to finance assets.

Table 2 also indicates that there is a concentration of assets among a small number of firms that is similar to the concentration of receipts displayed in *Table 1*. For example, 43% of S corporation assets are held by the largest 0.2% of firms, and 78% of partnership assets are held by the largest 1.1% of firms. Once again, the distribution is even more concentrated for corporations—98% of corporate assets are held by the largest 1.5% of firms. Thus, although only a small percentage of firms could be considered large for corporate tax purposes, they generate a significant amount of economic activity, and therefore possibly revenue.

Small Pass-Throughs and Corporations

While the analysis above focused on the similarities between large pass-throughs and corporations, there are similarities across pass-throughs and corporations more generally. Perhaps most notable, the majority of *both* pass-throughs and corporations are small, when measured by assets or receipts. The same data used to construct *Table 1* also show that over 95% of partnerships, S corporations, and C corporations generated receipts of less than $10 million.[14] Similarly, the data used in *Table 2* show that over 95% of S and C corporations and over 90% of partnerships have assets under $5 million.[15] The differing tax treatment of these smaller businesses raises the same efficiency and equity concerns that are part of the impetus for the current debate.

Addressing these concerns, however, would likely require a comprehensive reform of business taxation.

Estimated Number of Firms Affected

Estimates of the number of pass-throughs that could be taxed as corporations can be made by employing the same data used to construct *Table 1* and *Table 2*. Because those tables define size in two ways, two different sets of estimates are presented—one based on a receipt measure of size and a second based on an asset measure of size. Industry-specific estimates are also presented. The industry-level data needed to construct such estimates for partnerships based on an asset measure of size, however, are not available. Only asset-based estimates for S corporations are presented.

Aggregate Estimates

Table 3 displays the estimated number of partnerships and S corporations that could be subject to the corporate tax if size is measured by receipts. It is estimated that between 0.3% and 1.5% of all pass-throughs could be taxed as corporations if a receipt-based measure of size is used. In absolute terms, this corresponds to between 15,360 and 87,674 pass-throughs being subject to the corporate tax.

Table 3. Estimated Number of Pass-Throughs Potentially Taxed As Corporations Based on Receipts, 2003

	Over $10 Million		Over $50 Million	
	Firms	% of Total	Firms	% of Total
S corporations	62,655	1.9%	9,757	0.3%
Partnerships	25,019	1.1%	5,603	0.2%
Total	87,674	1.5%	15,360	0.3%

Source: CRS calculations using Internal Revenue Service's 2003 Statistics of Income (SOI) Integrated Business Database (IBD), table 2, http://www.irs.gov/pub/irs-soi/03ot2busbr.xls.

More S corporations than partnerships would be affected, in absolute and percentage terms, because S corporations tend to be larger on average than partnerships when size is measured by receipts. Between 0.3% and 1.9% (9,757 and 62,655) of S corporations could potentially be subject to the corporate tax, compared with 0.2% to 1.1% (5,603 and 25,019) of partnerships.

An asset-based measure of size produces similar estimates to those using a receipt-based measure.

Table 4 shows between 0.3% and 1.0% of all pass-throughs could be subject to the corporate tax depending on the asset threshold chosen to determine "large" firms. In contrast to the receipt-based estimates, using an asset-based measure of size results in more partnerships than S corporations being affected.

This is because partnerships tend to be larger (in terms of assets) than S corporations on average. Between 0.6% and 1.8% (18,180 to 57,524) of partnerships could potentially be subject to the corporate tax, compared with 0.08% to 0.4% (3,326 to 14,888) of S corporations.

Table 4. Estimated Number of Pass-Throughs Potentially Taxed As Corporations Based on Assets, 2008

	Over $25 Million		Over $50 Million		Over $100 Million	
	Firms	% of Total	Firms	% of Total	Firms	% of Total
S corporations	14,488	0.4%	6,937	0.2%	3,326	0.1%
Partnerships	57,524	1.8%	32,452	1.0%	18,180	0.6%
Total	72,012	1.0%	39,389	0.5%	21,506	0.3%

Source: CRS calculations using Internal Revenue Service, SOI, Table Wizard, http://www.taxstatstablewizard.com, and SOI, Partnership Statistics, http:// www. irs.gov/taxstats/bustaxstats/ article/0,,id=97153,00.html.

Table 3 and *Table 4* do not accurately describe the potential of the proposed policy change to obtain one of its objectives—raise tax revenue. While the estimates above suggest that only a relatively small fraction of pass-throughs could be subject to the corporate tax, they do not show the economic significance of the firms potentially affected.

The previous section, however, showed that the largest pass-throughs account for a disproportionate share of receipts, and held a disproportionate share of assets (see *Table 1* and *Table 2*).

Thus, while only a small number of firms may be impacted by the corporate tax, the revenue generated could potentially be significant since the affected firms would be large.

Industry-Level Estimates

It is also possible to estimate the number of firms in each industry that could potentially be subject to the corporate tax. *Table 5* displays the five industries that would likely be the most affected if large pass-throughs were taxed as corporations based on their receipts. The rankings were made based on the percentage of firms in each industry that would be affected if the size threshold were $10 million in receipts. There are 18 industry classifications in total. *Appendix A* contains estimates for all 18 industries.

Table 5. Five Industries Most Affected by Corporate Tax Based on Receipts, 2003

	Over $10 Million		*Over $50 Million*	
	Firms	*% of Industry*	*Firms*	*% of Industry*
S corporations:				
Manufacturing	9,443	6.30%	1,536	1.03%
Wholesale\retail trade	28,491	5.02%	5,508	0.97%
Mining	400	2.40%	50	0.30%
Transportation	2,273	2.20%	207	0.20%
Construction	9,581	2.14%	1,123	0.25%
Partnerships:				
Utilities	395	15.86%	211	8.47%
Manufacturing	2,756	6.83%	905	2.24%
Information	1,014	3.19%	360	1.13%
Wholesale\retail trade	5,028	2.94%	575	0.34%
Health care	1,571	2.90%	190	0.35%

Source: CRS calculations using Internal Revenue Service's 2003 Statistics of Income (SOI) Integrated Business Database (IBD), table 2, http://www.irs.gov/pub/irs-soi/03ot2busbr.xls.

Manufacturing and wholesale and retail trade would likely have the largest percentage of firms subject to the corporate tax among S corporations. It appears that over 5% of both industries would be taxed if the size threshold were set at $10 million, and just around 1% of both industries would be taxed if it were set at $50 million. Mining, transportation, and construction likely round out the top five S corporations, with about 2% being affected at the $10 million size cutoff, and 0.30% or less being taxed at a $50 million cutoff.

The utilities industries would likely be most affected among partnerships, followed by manufacturing. Nearly 16% of the utilities industry could pay the corporate tax if a $10 million threshold were used. Around 8.5% of the industry could pay the tax if the size limit were increased to $50 million. With respect to manufacturing, just under of 7% could be taxed as corporations if the smaller size definition were used, and just over 2% could pay the tax if the larger $50 million threshold were chosen. Information, wholesale and retail trade, and health care appear to make up the remaining top five most affected partnership industries.

Table 6. Five Industries Most Affected by Corporate Tax Based on Assets, 2008

	Over $25 Million		Over $50 Million		Over $100 Million	
	Firms	% of Industry	Firms	% of Industry	Firms	% of Industry
S corporations: Holding Companies	2,191	9.6%	1,706	7.4%	1,163	5.1%
Manufacturing	2361	1.5%	970	0.6%	416	0.3%
Mining	303	1.2%	153	0.6%	66	0.3%
Utilities	26	0.9%	15	0.5%	7	0.2%
Finance/Insurance	1,175	0.7%	712	0.4%	377	0.2%

Source: CRS calculations using Internal Revenue Service, SOI, Table Wizard, http://www.taxstatstablewizard.com, and SOI, Partnership Statistics, http://www.irs.gov/taxstats/bustaxstats/ article/0,,id=97153,00.html.

Industry-level estimates of the number of firms that could be affected if an asset-based measure of size were used are presented in *Table 6.* Industry estimates can only be made for S corporations, however, since industry-level data on partnership asset holdings do not exist. The rankings were made based on the percentage of firms in each industry that would be affected if the size threshold were $25 million in assets. *Appendix B* provide estimates for all 18 industry classifications.

It is estimated that holding companies would be most affected.[16] Between 5.1% and 9.6% of S corporation holding companies could be subject to the corporate tax depending on the asset threshold used. Manufacturing ranks second, with between 0.3% and 1.5% of S corporations in the industry potentially affected. Mining, utilities, and the finance and insurance industry appear to round out the top five. *Table 6* also indicates that as the size threshold increases, the number of potentially affected firms across industries falls. For the largest size measure, the number of firms falls to less than 2% for all industries except holding companies.

Lastly, comparing *Table 5* and *Table 6* reveals that the measure of size used matters for determining what industries will be affected the most. For example, while holding companies are estimated as the most affected if an asset-based measure of size is used, the industry does not even break the top five if a receipt-based measure of size is used. The decision about how to measure size becomes less important as the minimum size used to determine which firms would be subject to the corporate tax increases. For instance, aside from S corporation holding companies, if a $100 million asset threshold were used, no industry would see more than 0.3% of firms taxed as corporations. If a $50 million receipt threshold were used, only two industries would have more than 0.3% of firms paying the corporate tax.

POLICY CHOICES AND CONSIDERATIONS

Congress will face a number of policy choices and considerations should it choose to tax large pass-throughs as corporations. One choice would concern the size of a pass-through that would trigger the corporate tax. This involves two steps. First, a measure of business size would need to be chosen. Two measures were used in this report—an asset-based measure and a receipt-based measure. Alternatives to these two options include a profit-based measure, an employment-based measure, a composite measure (i.e., based on assets, receipts, and employment), or industry specific measures (e.g., an asset-based measure for certain industries, and a receipt-based measure for other industries).

An asset-based measure has some attractive features. Assets are likely to be more stable over the business cycle than revenues, profits, and employment. Therefore, using an asset-based measure would help to reduce uncertainty about how a business will be taxed in any given year. It may also be harder for pass-throughs to manipulate their assets to avoid being labeled as large. The most sophisticated pass-throughs may be able to shift revenue or income to subsidiaries located outside the U.S. in an attempt to avoid the corporate tax. At the same time, certain firms may still be able to strategically shift assets out of the country to avoid the corporate tax. There is some evidence that firms with extensive intangible assets (e.g., patients, copy rights, trademarks, etc.), such as those in the pharmaceutical industry, and the computer and electronic equipment industry, may be engaged in this behavior.[17]

An asset-based measure of size, however, may not accurately measure the economic size of businesses in particular industries. Certain firms and industries may be less capital intensive than others and therefore have fewer assets.

For example, the manufacturing and mining industries will naturally have more assets than the health care industry, or the education industry because these two industries are more service-oriented.

Particular health care and education firms could still be considered large if measured by receipts, profits, or employment, but may not be classified as such when measured by assets.

An alternative to using a single measure of size would be to use a composite measure of size that is based on assets, employment, and revenue or income.

Another option would be to use industry specific measures, such as an asset-based measure for the manufacturing industry, and a receipt or profit-based measure for the health care industry. In any case, if policymakers decide to use a measure based on receipts, profits, or employment, they may want to consider using an multi-year moving average since these measure may fluctuate substantially from year to year.

The second step in defining "large" pass-throughs is choosing a threshold above which a pass-through would be taxed as a corporation. The Obama Administration may be considering a proposal that would define a large pass-through as one earning $50 million or more in receipts.[18]

The Administration has also considered using an industry-specific threshold to impose a financial crisis responsibility fee on large financial institutions. This threshold would be asset based and set at $50 billion, which would be suitable for indentifying large financial institutions.[19] However, such a threshold may exclude firms in other industries that are considered large by alternative measures. One way to address this would be to employ industry-specific size thresholds. In determining the thresholds, Congress could direct the IRS to develop appropriate industry specific thresholds, or rely on methods similar to those already implemented by the Small Business Administration (SBA).

Alternatively, Congress could specifically legislate the size measures and thresholds to be used to decide which pass-throughs must pay the corporate tax.[20]

Congress could also opt to exempt pass-throughs in certain industries. Again, though, economic theory generally calls for uniform tax treatment across industries, although differential tax treatment may be justified when the actions of firms in certain industries bestow benefits to or impose costs on society that are not reflected in market prices. Examples include research and development (benefit or positive spillover) and pollution (cost or negative spillover).

Still, it would probably be more efficient to levy a uniform income tax and then use more precise policy tools (e.g., credits, deductions, grants, regulation, etc.) to target spillovers at the firm level. Additionally, by including all industries and thus broadening the corporate tax base as much as possible, corporate tax rates could potentially be reduced further, which may be more efficient and equitable than if certain industries were excluded.

Unfortunately, economic analysis does not provide any insight into the appropriate threshold used to define large firms. Economic theory would tend to suggest that any business tax system should tax all businesses—large and small—equally.

The analysis in this report, particularly *Table 3* and *Table 4*, however, does provide estimates of the number of firms that would be subject to the corporate tax if particular size thresholds were chosen. These figures provide policymakers with a starting point from which to construct a more formal proposal if they should choose to do so.

CONCLUSION

This report used aggregate and industry-level individual tax return data to analyze how many partnerships and S corporations could be subject to the corporate tax.

The analysis determined that if a receipt-based measure of size is used, then between 0.3% and 1.5% of S corporations and partnerships could be taxed as corporations depending on the definition of a "large" passthrough—either receipts exceeding \$50 million or \$10 million. Using an asset-based measure of size produces similar estimates.

It is estimated that between 0.3% and 1.0% of pass-throughs could pay the corporate tax depending on whether a \$100 million or \$25 million asset threshold is used to define a "large" firm. Although estimates suggest that only a small percentage of passthroughs could be considered large for corporate tax purposes, the affected firms are responsible for a significant amount of economic activity, indicating that the proposed policy change could potentially raise substantial revenue.

Appendix A. Industry-Level Estimates Using a Receipts-Based Measure of Size

Table A-1. Estimated Number of S Corporations Potentially Taxed as Corporations Based on Business Receipts, 2003

	Over $10 Million		*Over $50 Million*	
Industry	*Firms*	*% of Industry*	*Firms*	*% of Industry*
Manufacturing	9,443	6.30%	1,536	1.03%
Wholesale\retail trade	28,491	5.02%	5,508	0.97%
Mining	400	2.40%	50	0.30%
Transportation	2,273	2.20%	207	0.20%
Construction	9,581	2.14%	1,123	0.25%
Holding companies	378	1.69%	29	0.13%
Information	950	1.42%	104	0.16%
Waste management	1,687	1.00%	263	0.16%
Finance and insurance	1,157	0.86%	155	0.11%
Utilities	24	0.82%	13	0.44%
Agriculture, forestry, fishing, and hunting	583	0.72%	85	0.10%
Educational services	185	0.67%	12	0.04%
Health care	1,349	0.65%	211	0.10%
Professional, scientific, and technical services	3,149	0.61%	216	0.04%
Arts, entertainment, and recreation	401	0.54%	52	0.07%
Accommodation, food services, and drinking places	1,008	0.54%	92	0.05%
Real estate	1,065	0.29%	73	0.02%
Other services	531	0.27%	28	0.01%

Source: CRS calculations.

Table A-2. Estimated Number of Partnerships Potentially Taxed as Corporations Based on Business Receipts, 2003

	Over $10 Million		*Over $50 Million*	
Industry	*Firms*	*% of Industry*	*Firms*	*% of Industry*
Utilities	395	15.86%	211	8.47%
Manufacturing	2,756	6.83%	905	2.24%
Information	1,014	3.19%	360	1.13%
Wholesale\retail trade	5,028	2.94%	575	0.34%
Health care	1,571	2.90%	190	0.35%
Construction	3,008	2.14%	456	0.32%
Transportation	564	1.89%	144	0.48%
Mining	512	1.82%	132	0.47%
Accommodation, food services, and drinking places	1,293	1.59%	151	0.19%
Holding companies	335	1.55%	91	0.42%
Professional, scientific, and technical services	1,950	1.29%	471	0.31%
Finance and insurance	3,020	1.17%	682	0.26%
Waste management	424	0.97%	97	0.22%
Arts, entertainment, and recreation	355	0.82%	120	0.28%
Educational services	29	0.32%	6	0.07%
Agriculture, forestry, fishing, and hunting	369	0.30%	70	0.06%
Real estate	2,309	0.21%	256	0.02%
Other services	82	0.13%	24	0.04%

Source: CRS calculations.

Appendix B. Industry-Level Estimates Using An Asset-Based Measure of Size

Table B-1. Estimated Number of S Corporations Potentially Taxed as Corporations by Industry Based on Assets, 2008rations Potentially Taxed As Corporations by Industry Based on Assets, 2008

	Over $25 Million		*Over $50 Million*		*Over $100 Million*	
Industry	*Firms*	*% of Industry*	*Firms*	*% of Industr y*	*Firms*	*% of Industr y*
Holding companies	2,191	9.56%	1,706	7.4%	1,163	5.08%
Manufacturing	2,361	1.46%	153	0.6%	66	0.26%
Mining	303	1.21%	970	0.6%	416	0.26%
Utilities	26	0.92%	15	0.5%	7	0.25%
Finance/insurance	1,175	0.72%	712	0.4%	377	0.23%
Wholesale and retail trade	3,186	0.49%	1,209	0.19%	453	0.07%
Construction	2,088	0.37%	827	0.14%	292	0.05%
Agriculture, forestry, fishing, and hunting	278	0.34%	129	0.16%	54	0.07%
Information	235	0.32%	114	0.15%	51	0.07%
Transportation and warehousing	333	0.26%	158	0.12%	72	0.06%
Real estate	1,208	0.26%	470	0.10%	176	0.04%
Arts/ entertainment	152	0.17%	69	0.08%	40	0.04%
Waste Management	186	0.09%	95	0.05%	37	0.02%
Accommodation and food service	194	0.09%	84	0.04%	33	0.02%
Educational services	31	0.08%	12	0.03%	4	0.01%
Professional, scientific, and technical services	387	0.06%	149	0.02%	61	0.01%
Health care	110	0.04%	45	0.02%	18	0.01%
Other services	42	0.02%	18	0.01%	5	0.00%

Source: CRS calculations.

End Notes

[1] Nicola M. White and Drew Pierson, "Baucus Says Congress Should Look at Taxing Passthroughs as Corporations," Tax Notes Today, May 5, 2011.

[2] See Senate hearing testimony by Treasury Secretary Timothy Geithner. U.S. Congress, Senate Committee on Finance, The President's Budget for Fiscal Year 2012, 112th Cong., February 16, 2011.

[3] A Joint Report by the White House and the Department of the Treasury Department, The President's Framework for Business Tax Reform, Washington, DC, February 2012, p. 10, http://www.treasury.gov/resource-center/tax-policy/Documents/The-Presidents-Framework-for-Business-Tax-Reform-02-22-2012.pdf.

[4] Bernie Becker, "Members eager for White House tax plan," The Hill, May 4, 2011, Online edition, http://thehill.com/ business-a-lobbying/159351-lawmakers-eager-for-white-house-tax-plan-.

[5] The income of a pass-through income can be subject to the corporate tax if the pass-through is a subsidiary of a corporate parent.

[6] For more information on the taxation of various business forms, see CRS Report R40748, Business Organizational Choices: Taxation and Responses to Legislative Changes, by Mark P. Keightley.

[7] Sullivan estimates that gross corporate tax revenues would be $40 billion higher if the corporate sector's share of business activity remained the same as it was in 1999. Assuming the corporate sector's share of business activity remained the same as it was in 1990, Sullivan estimates that gross corporate tax revenues would be $140 billion higher. Since the shift from corporate to pass-through form implies that businesses are generating more tax revenue under the individual income tax, the above figures do not represent the net revenue loss to the federal government. Sullivan states that "back-of-the-envelope calculations suggest that the net revenue loss to the government is probably more like one-third of the gross figure." Multiplying $40 billion and $140 billion by one third produces the figures cited above. Martin A. Sullivan , "Passthroughs Shrink the Corporate Tax by $140 Billion," Tax Notes, February 28, 2011, pp. 987- 989.

[8] Nearly all major tax reform proposal released recently have called for some kind of base broadening which can be used to reduce tax rates with the aim of improving the business tax environment. The President's Economic Recovery and Advisory Board specifically calls for examining the distinction between corporate and non-corporate forms, along with general base broadening, lower tax rates, and reduced complexity. See, President's Economic Recovery and Advisory Board, The Report on Tax Reform Options: Simplicity, Compliance, and Corporate Taxation, Washington, DC, August 2010, http://www.whitehouse.gov/sites/default/files/microsites/PERAB_Tax_Reform_Report.pdf. For a summary of other recent tax reform proposals see, CRS Report R41591, Tax Reform: An Overview of Proposals in the 112th Congress, by James M. Bickley. On March 7, 2012, the House Committee on Ways and Means held a hearing on the issue of pass-throughs taxation in the context of tax reform. Testimony given at that hearing may be found at http://waysandmeans.house.gov/Calendar/EventSingle.aspx?EventID=282644.

[9] See Jane G. Gravelle, The Economic Effects of Taxing Capital Income (MIT Press, 1994), pp. 77-82, and James B. Mackie, "Unfinished Business of the 1986 Tax Reform Act: An Effective Tax Rate Analysis of Current Issues in the Taxation of Capital Income," National Tax Journal, vol. 55, no. 2 (June 2002), pp. 293-337.

[10] CRS Report R41743, International Corporate Tax Rate Comparisons and Policy Implications, by Jane G. Gravelle.

[11] In 1992, The Department of the Treasury drafted a 268 page report containing a comprehensive analysis of corporate and individual tax integration. See, The Department of the Treasury, Integration of the Individual and Corporate Tax Systems: Taxing Business Income Once, Washington, DC, January 1992, http://www.treasury.gov/resource-center/tax-policy/Documents/integration.pdf. For a summary of the Treasury report, see R. Glenn Hubbard, "Corporate Tax Integration: A View from the Treasury Department," Journal of Economic Perspectives, vol. 7, no. 1 (Winter 1993), pp. 115-132.

[12] Sole proprietors are responsible for the remaining share of business income.

[13] Prior to TRA86, the highest individual income tax rate was 50%, whereas the highest corporate income tax rate was 46%. TRA86 eventually lowered the highest individual tax rate to 28% and the highest corporate tax rate to 34%. An IRS study found that the more favorable tax treatment under the individual tax schedule after TRA86 induced certain businesses organized as C corporations to reorganize as S corporations. See Susan M. Whittman and Amy Gill, "S Corporation Elections After the Tax Reform Act of 1986," SOI Bulletin, publication 1136 (Spring 1998).

[14] Author's calculations using 2003 SOI data.

[15] Author's calculations using 2008 SOI data.

[16] A holding company owns other businesses which may produce goods or provide services, although the holding company itself does not. Included in the holding company industry are bank, financial, and insurance holding companies, as well as public utility holding companies and others.

[17] See CRS Report R40623, Tax Havens: International Tax Avoidance and Evasion, by Jane G. Gravelle for a discussion of intangible asset transfers and corporate tax avoidance.

[18] Martin A. Sullivan, "Why Not Tax Large Passthroughs as Corporations," Tax Notes, June 6, 2011, pp. 1015-1018.

[19] Office of Management and Budget, Analytical United States Government,, Washington, DC, February 13, 2012, p. 204, http://www.whitehouse.gov/sites/default/files/ Perspectives, Federal Receipts, Budget of the omb/budget/ fy2013/assets/receipts.pdf.

[20] For more information on the SBA, see CRS Report RL33243, Small Business Administration: A Primer on Programs, by Robert Jay Dilger.

In: Business Taxation
Editors: J. C. Teague and K. Fawner
ISBN: 978-1-62257-998-3

Chapter 4

Who Earns Pass-Through Business Income? An Analysis of Individual Tax Return Data*

Mark P. Keightley

Summary

Pass-through businesses——sole proprietorships, partnerships, and S corporations——generate more than half of all business income in the United States. Pass-through income is, in general, taxed only once at the individual income tax rates when it is distributed to its owners. In contrast, the income of C corporations is taxed twice; once at the corporate level according to corporate tax rates, and then a second time at the individual tax rates when shareholders receive dividend payments or realize capital gains. This leads to the so-called ""double taxation"" of corporate profits.

This report analyzes individual tax return data to determine who earns pass-through business income and bears the burden of taxes on that income. The analysis finds that over 82% of net pass-through income is earned by taxpayers with an adjusted gross income (AGI) over $100,000, although these taxpayers account for just 23% of returns filed. A significant fraction of pass-through income is concentrated among upper-

* This is an edited, reformatted and augmented version of a Congressional Research Service publication, CRS Report for Congress R42359, from www.crs.gov, prepared for Members and Committees of Congress, dated February 16, 2012.

income earners. Taxpayers with AGI over $250,000, for example, receive 62% of pass-through income, but account for just over 6% of returns with pass-through income. A closer look at S corporations and partnerships shows passive income accounts for 10% and 25%, respectively, of their total income. This analysis, when combined with research on the corporate tax burden, suggests that higher-income taxpayers will generally bear most of the burden from increased pass-through taxes.

A number of proposed and scheduled tax changes would result in pass-throughs paying higher taxes. Several lawmakers and the Obama Administration, for example, have expressed interest in taxing large pass-throughs as corporations, which would subject some pass-throughs to an additional layer of taxation. Pass-through taxation could also increase if a tax reform that includes lower corporate tax rates that are paid for by the elimination or reduction of certain business tax benefits is enacted. Additionally, the scheduled expiration of the 2001/2003 tax cuts at the end of this year could increase taxes on pass-throughs by increasing individual tax rates. Lastly, a new 3.8% tax on passive income that was enacted as part of the Health Care and Education Reconciliation Act of 2010 (HCERA, P.L. 111-152) is set to take effect in 2013. The tax may apply to some pass-throughs.

While the analysis of these proposed and scheduled changes suggests that higher-income taxpayers will generally bear most of the burden from increased pass-through taxes, there are circumstances that could raise congressional concern. For example, an across-the-board expiration of the 2001/2003 individual tax rates will increase taxes for all pass-through owners. One option for preventing the tax burden from increasing for lower and middle class business owners is to allow the reduced rates to expire only for higher-income earners.

Concern has also risen over the new 3.8% tax on passive income and its effect on pass-throughs. The distributional analysis in this report shows, however, most S corporation and partnership income is the active type, and active business income is exempt from the 3.8% tax. The share of income that is passive, and potentially subject to the new tax, overwhelmingly accrues to higher-income taxpayers——77% of passive partnership income and 93% of passive S corporation income went to taxpayers with AGI over $250,000. Sole proprietors could generally be expected to be exempt from the tax since most of their income is likely active.

INTRODUCTION

More than half of business income is generated by sole proprietorships, partnerships, and S corporations.[1] This fact is important because the income of these businesses is, in general, taxed only once at the individual income tax rates when it is distributed to its owners. This has led sole proprietorships, partnerships, and S corporations to be referred to as ""“pass-throughs”"" since their income ""“passes through”"" the business to its owners.[2] In contrast, the income of C corporations is taxed twice; once at the corporate level according to corporate tax rates, and then a second time at the individual tax rates when shareholders receive dividend payments or realize capital gains. This leads to the so-called ""“double taxation”"" of corporate profits.[3]

A number of proposed and scheduled tax changes could result in pass-throughs paying higher taxes. Several lawmakers and the Obama Administration, for example, have expressed interest in taxing large pass-throughs as corporations, which would subject some of these entities to an additional layer of taxation. Pass-through taxation could also increase if one of the proposed tax reform plans that call for lower corporate tax rates paid for by the elimination or reduction of certain business tax benefits is enacted. Additionally, the scheduled expiration of the 2001/2003 tax cuts at the end of this year could increase taxes on pass-throughs. Lastly, a new 3.8% “unearned income Medicare contribution” ” tax that is set to take effect in 2013 may apply to some pass-throughs.

This report uses a nationally representative sample of tax returns to analyze who earns pass-through income.[4] The analysis finds that upper-income earners account for the majority of pass-through income earned, although lower- and middle-income taxpayers account for the majority of pass-through returns filed. The analysis then determines who would bear the burden of increased taxes on pass-throughs. Theoretically, it is possible that higher-income pass-through owners could shift the burden of increased taxes to lower- and middle-income employees by reducing wages or employment. The analysis on who earns pass-through income, when combined with research on the corporate tax burden, however, suggests that most of the tax burden would fall on higher-income taxpayers. A more detailed discussion of the proposed and scheduled tax changes is presented before moving on to the analysis.

PROPOSED AND SCHEDULED TAX CHANGES

A number of recent proposals could increase taxes for pass-throughs. In early 2011, Senate Finance Committee Chairman Max Baucus suggested, for example, that pass-throughs earning above a certain income might have to be taxed as corporations.[5] That same year, while testifying before the Senate

Finance Committee, Treasury Secretary Tim Geithner said ““Congress has to revisit this basic question about whether it makes sense for us as a country to allow certain businesses to choose whether they’’re treated as corporations for tax purposes or not.””[6] The Treasury Secretary’’s comments seemed to indicate his concern about large pass-throughs that were paying lower taxes by intentionally choosing not to be taxed as a corporation. The Secretary’’s comments also appear to resonate with reports that the Administration is developing a proposal to tax large pass-throughs as corporations, as well as consistent with a broad proposal made by the President’’s Economic Recovery Advisory Board to tax pass-throughs with corporate characteristics as corporations.[7]

Recent proposals by lawmakers and the Administration to reform the corporate tax code have called for lower corporate tax rates paid for by the elimination or reduction of certain corporate tax benefits, which could affect pass-throughs.[8] Pass-throughs would generally not benefit from a reduction in corporate tax rates, since their income is not subject to the corporate tax. Additionally, depending on how corporate tax benefits are scaled back to offset a rate reduction, pass-throughs could see their tax burden increase. The reason is that not all ““““corporate”””” tax benefits are exclusively available to corporations. Often they are available to business more generally.[9]

Scheduled tax changes that could potentially affect pass-throughs include the expiration of the 2001/2003 tax cuts, later extended in 2010, that is set to occur at the end of 2012. Specifically, barring congressional action, the current individual tax rate structure of 10%, 15% 25%, 28%, 33%, and 35% will revert to 15%, 28%, 31%, 36%, and 39.6%. Since ordinary pass-through income is taxed according to individual rates, some owners of pass-through businesses would likely experience an increase in taxes owed.[10] A number of pass-through business owners who realize capital gains, including hedge fund managers who realize carried interest income, could also see taxes increase if the reduced rates for long-term capital gains are also allowed to expire.[11]

The other scheduled tax change that may affect pass-throughs is a new 3.8% ““unearned income Medicare contribution”” tax set to take effect in 2013.[12] Specifically, the Health Care and Education Reconciliation Act of 2010 (HCERA, P.L. 111-152) included a 3.8% tax on the passive income of those with incomes over $250,000 (couples) and $200,000 (singles). The tax is limited to the excess of income over these amounts or total passive income, whichever is smaller. Active business income is excluded from the tax. There is concern in the business community that this tax may negatively affect pass-through business owners who earn passive business income.[13]

WHO EARNS PASS-THROUGH BUSINESS INCOME?

Approximately 27 million (or one in five) taxpayers reported pass-through business income (or loss) totaling more than $704 billion in 2006. Among those earning pass-through income, the average amount reported was $26,011. These figures exclude capital gains income from passthroughs and farming income. This section analyzes the distribution of pass-through income by a measure of taxpayer income that is used for tax purposes——adjusted gross income (AGI). When useful and possible, the analysis also distinguishes between sole proprietorship, partnership, and S corporation income, as well as active and passive income.

Figure 1 shows the distribution of pass-through income by AGI class. A more detailed distribution, along with the distribution of tax returns reporting pass-through income, may be found in *Table A-1* of the *Appendix.* Taxpayers with income of $100,000 or greater earned 82% of pass-through income, while accounting for roughly 23% of returns reporting pass-through income. Conversely, taxpayers with AGI less than $100,000 earned about 18% of pass-through income, but accounted for 77% of returns with pass-through income. A significant proportion of pass-through income was concentrated among upper-income earners. Taxpayers with AGI over $250,000, for example, received 62% of pass-through income, but accounted for just over 6% of returns reporting such income. Millionaires earned about 35% of pass-through income, while filing roughly 1% of all returns with pass-through income.

Table 1 displays the distribution of pass-through income by business type. The distribution shows that sole proprietorship income was more evenly distributed across income groups than partnership and S corporation income. Partnership net income was more concentrated among upper income individuals with nearly all of it accruing to taxpayers with AGI in excess of $100,000, including nearly 44% accruing to those with AGI over $1 million. S corporation income was also concentrated at the upper-end of the distribution, although more so than partnership income. For example, while nearly all of S corporation income accrued to taxpayers with income over $100,000, a greater share went to those with AGI over $1 million than with partnership income——about 58%.

Table 1 also shows a concentration of net losses for partnerships and S corporations at the lower end of the income distribution. Pass-through income and losses are one component of AGI. Thus, if a taxpayer relies primarily on a partnership or S corporation for income, and the business realizes losses, the taxpayer's AGI will likely be negative.

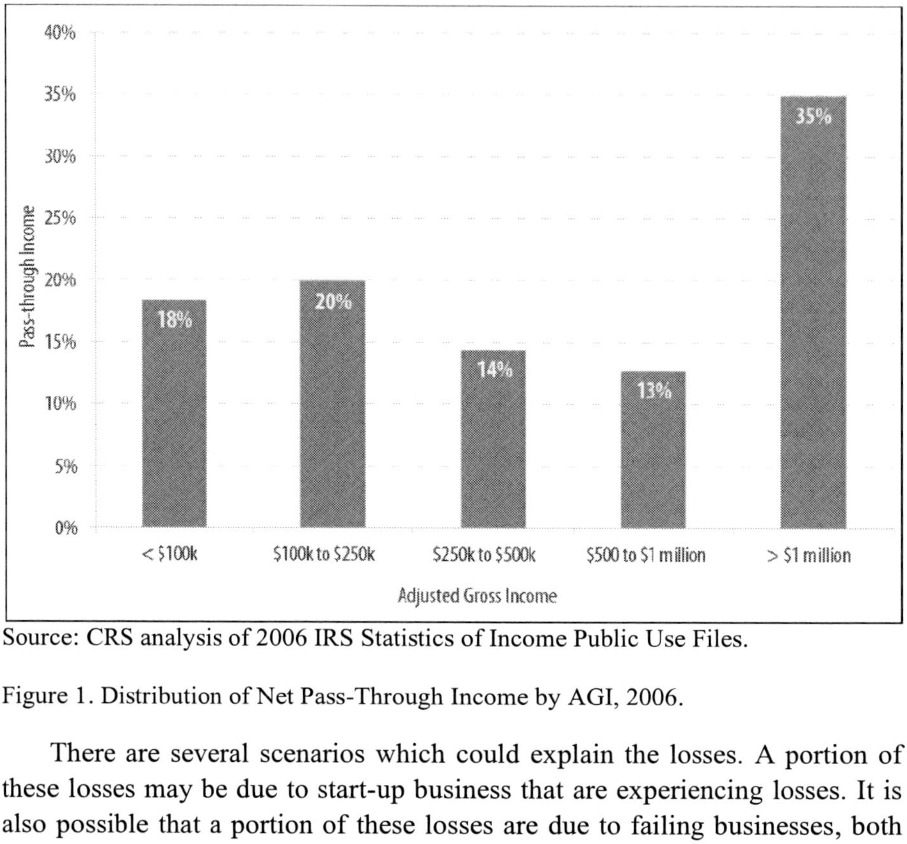

Source: CRS analysis of 2006 IRS Statistics of Income Public Use Files.

Figure 1. Distribution of Net Pass-Through Income by AGI, 2006.

There are several scenarios which could explain the losses. A portion of these losses may be due to start-up business that are experiencing losses. It is also possible that a portion of these losses are due to failing businesses, both new and old. Lastly, some of the losses may be attributable to temporary business disruptions experienced at particular firms. Without more detailed data on the businesses associated with these losses, however, its difficult to know for certain. The individual data do show that for most taxpayers at this end of the distribution, partnership and S corporation losses were larger than non pass-through income, indicating that these taxpayers were relying primarily on pass-through income. Partnership and S corporation income can be separated into active and passive income. The distinction between the two can be important because passive activity losses rules generally prevent passive losses from offsetting active income. Active income is income resulting from active participation in a business, whereas passive income is income from a business that the taxpayer did not materially participate in. A business partner involved in the day to day management and operations of the business, for example, would earn active income, while a silent partner who has no involvement in the business outside of possibly financial commitments would earn passive income. Sole proprietorship income is not distinguished in the data used in this analysis. Most sole proprietors, however, will be actively involved in their business (since they are sole owner) suggesting that the overwhelming majority of sole proprietor income is active.

Table 1. Distribution of Net Pass-Through Income by Business Type and AGI, 2006

Adjusted Gross Income	Sole Proprietorships	Partnerships	S Corporations
< $10k	2.12%	-11.30%	-5.84%
$10k to $20k	8.88%	0.19%	-0.08%
$20k to $30k	6.72%	0.54%	0.07%
$30k to $40k	4.84%	1.14%	0.33%
$40k to $50k	4.98%	0.74%	0.45%
$50k to $75k	10.62%	2.31%	1.94%
$75 to $100k	9.27%	2.76%	2.72%
$100k to $250k	26.65%	15.62%	13.95%
$250k to $500k	11.74%	20.45%	13.83%
$500k to $1 million	5.57%	23.72%	14.25%
> $1 million	8.60%	43.84%	58.37%
Total	100%	100%	100%
Highest Earners			
$1 million - $2 million	2.70%	16.40%	14.77%
$2 million - $5 million	4.53%	14.24%	15.95%
$5 million - $10 million	0.52%	5.64%	8.86%
> $10 million	0.86%	7.56%	18.79%
Total	8.62%	43.84%	58.37%

Source: CRS analysis of 2006 IRS Statistics of Income Public Use Files.

Figure 2 displays the distribution of active and passive income for partnerships and S corporations. As Figure 2 shows, passive income accounts for 10% of total S corporation income, and 25% of partnership income. Conversely, 90% of S corporation income and 75% of partnership income is active. A significant share of passive income from either business type is concentrated among higher income individuals (see Table A-2 in the Appendix).

WHO WOULD BEAR THE TAX BURDEN?

The analysis above found that the majority of pass-through income accrues to higher income earners.

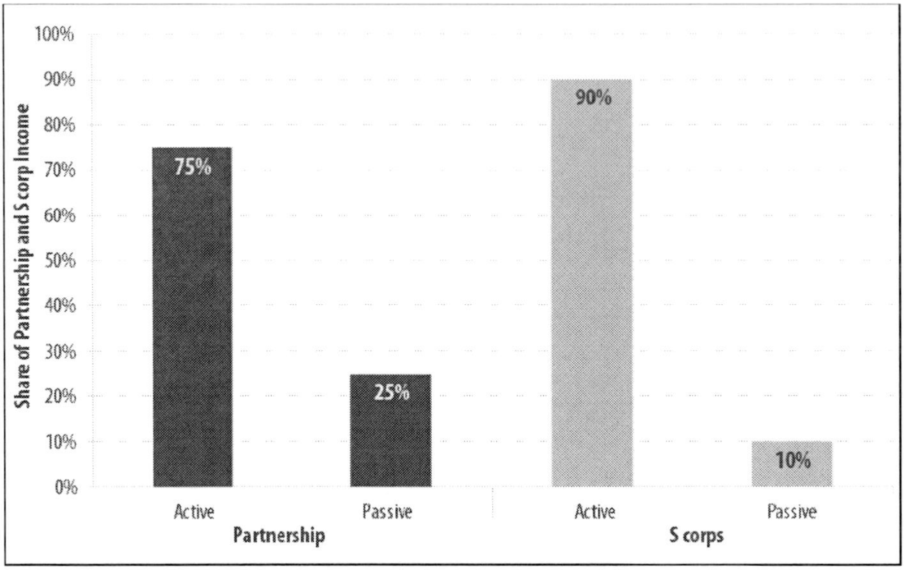

Source: CRS analysis of 2006 IRS Statistics of Income Public Use Files.

Note: The passive income measure used here does not include capital gains. The data do not allow for corporate and non corporate capital gains to be separated. Aggregate data show that capital gains are a significant income source for pass-through owners, which indicates the distributions presented could change non trivially if they could be included.

Figure 2. Distribution of Active and Passive Income by Business Type, 2006.

The income these individuals receive is the result of an ownership stake in either a sole proprietorship, partnership, or S corporation. But there are other taxpayers, namely the employees at these firms, who receive income from pass-throughs as well. If taxes are increased on passthroughs, it is possible that pass-through owners could lower wages, scale back benefits, or reduce employment in an effort to reduce the burden of the tax increase on themselves. Thus, although the majority of pass-through income is concentrated at the upper-end of the income distribution, the tax burden could be shared with lower- and middle-income taxpayers who work at these businesses.

Research on who bears the corporate tax burden can be utilized to understand who would bear the burden of increased pass-through taxation generally——owners (capital), or workers (labor).[14] The traditional analysis of the corporate tax indicates that it is capital that bears the burden. In contrast, a number of more recent theoretical studies find labor bearing the majority of the corporate tax burden. These results, however, appear to rely critically on particular assumptions (e.g., an open economy with highly mobile capital) which drive the results. When these assumptions are relaxed the burden of the corporate tax is found to fall mostly on capital, in line with the traditional analysis.[15]

There has also been a resurgent empirical interest in determining the incidence of the corporate tax. A number of recent empirical studies have found that majority of the corporate tax burden falls on labor. These studies are reviewed and critiqued in CRS Report RL34229, *Corporate Tax Reform: Issues for Congress*, by Jane G. Gravelle and Thomas L. Hungerford, who find the research is seriously flawed, produces unreasonable estimates, is not robust (sensitive to specification changes), or is inconsistent with theory. Given the unreliability of recent empirical research, and the consistency of traditional theoretical models, Gravelle and Hungerford conclude that it "“appears that most of the burden of the corporate tax falls on capital.”" [16] Thus, combining the corporate tax burden research with the analysis of who earns pass-through income, it seems likely that an increased pass-through tax burden would fall mostly on higher-income taxpayers.

Policy Concerns and Options

There are several potential concerns that Congress may want to consider regarding increased taxes on pass-throughs. In some cases there may be options for alleviating these concerns. In other cases it appears that the concerns may not be validated by the data. The following discusses several circumstances that commonly elicit policy concerns.

While it appears as a general rule of thumb that higher-income business owners would bear most of the burden from increased pass-through taxation, there still may be concern about lower- and middle-income pass-through owners. For example, an across-the-board expiration of the 2001/2003 individual tax rates will increase taxes for all pass-through owners. One option for preventing the tax burden from increasing for lower and middle class business owners is to allow the reduced rates to expire only for higher-income earners. Estimates suggest a small share (3% or so) of businesses would be affected if the top individual rates were to expire.[17]

Similarly, there could be concern over the effect on lower and middle income pass-through owners from tax reform plans that call for lower corporate tax rates to be paid for by the elimination or reduction of certain "corporate" tax benefits. Scaling back corporate tax benefits, however, could raise taxes for pass-throughs since a number of corporate tax benefits are actually available to businesses more generally. An option for preventing the reduction of business tax benefits from impacting these businesses is to allow them to continue to claim the benefits. Additionally, a number of the benefits that have been considered as offsets could be reduced or eliminated without affecting smaller pass-throughs since they generally benefit corporations——including provisions related to overseas operations and fossil fuels.[18]

Lastly, there is concern that the new 3.8% unearned income Medicare contribution tax may negatively affect many small businesses.[19] As the distributional analysis showed, however, most S corporation and partnership income is the active type, and active business income is exempt from the 3.8% tax. The share of income that is passive, and potentially subject to the new tax, overwhelmingly accrues to higher income taxpayers——77% of passive partnership income and 93% of passive S corporation income accrued to taxpayers with AGI over $250,000. Passive income earned by those with AGI of less than $200,000 (single) or $250,000 (married) would not be taxed since these taxpayers' income is not high enough to trigger the tax. Sole proprietors could generally be expected to be exempt from the tax since most of their income is likely active. It should be noted that there is one particular limitation of the data when it comes to analyzing the 3.8% tax on unearned income. The data do not allow for pass-through capital gains to be distinguished from corporate capital gains. Capital gains are considered passive income for purposes of the 3.8% tax and could be a significant income source for some pass-through owners, particularly for hedge fund managers who receive carried interest. Thus, although most ordinary pass-through income is active, pass-through owners do receive other income which is passive. Still, it is likely that if capital gains could be isolated, the distribution of capital gains would be even more concentrated among higher-income taxpayers since investment income is generally concentrated among this group. In this case, the burden of the 3.8% tax would, like pass-through taxes more generally, fall on higher-income taxpayers.

CONCLUSION

This report analyzed individual tax return data to determine who earns pass-through business income. It determined that most pass-through income is earned by higher-income individuals, although most returns reporting pass-through income are filed by lower- and middle-income individuals. The report then analyzed who would bear the burden from increased taxes on pass-through income as a result of several proposed and scheduled tax changes. Given the distribution of pass-through income, and applying research about the incidence of the corporate tax, it seems likely that in general an increase in pass-through taxes would fall mostly on higher-income taxpayers. In circumstances where there is concern that this may not be true, the report identifies options to prevent lower and middle class pass-through owners from experiencing an increase in taxes.

APPENDIX. DETAILED DISTRIBUTIONS

Table A-1. Distribution of Tax Returns and Pass-Through Income by Adjusted Gross Income, 2006

Adjusted Gross Income	Returns Reporting Pass-Through Income	% of Returns Reporting Pass-Through Income	Total Pass-Through Income	% of Total Pass-Through Income	Average Pass-Through Income
< $10k	4,478,554	16.53%	$ -26.6	-3.78%	-$5,945
$10k to $20k	3,583,598	13.23%	$ 25.6	3.63%	$7,142
$20k - $30k	2,396,688	8.85%	$ 20.3	2.89%	$8,482
$30k - $40k	2,004,143	7.40%	$ 16.5	2.34%	$8,255
$40k - $50k	1,891,013	6.98%	$ 16.6	2.36%	$8,786
$50k - $75k	3,951,384	14.59%	$ 39.2	5.57%	$9,909
$75 - $100k	2,684,429	9.91%	$ 38.0	5.39%	$14,170
$100k - $250k	4,370,055	16.13%	$137.2	19.45%	$31,398
$250k - $500k	1,026,149	3.79%	$101.5	14.48%	$98,968
$500k - $1 million	416,344	1.54%	$ 89.8	12.75%	$215,922
> $1 million	288,175	1.06%	$246.4	34.92%	$854,943
Total	27,090,675	100.0%	$704.4	100.0%	$26,011
Highest Earners					
$1 million - $2 million	167,754	0.62%	$72.1	10.22%	$429,367
$2 million - $5 million	83,776	0.31%	$76.9	10.93%	$918,840
$5 million - $10 million	22,068	0.08%	$33.6	4.77%	$1,524,106
> $10 million	14,577	0.05%	$63.8	9.06%	$4,373,348
Total	288,175	1.06%	$246.4	34.92%	$855,064

Source: CRS analysis of 2006 IRS Statistics of Income Public Use Files. Note: Averages are conditional on having pass-through income.

Table A-2. Distribution of Active and Passive Partnership and S Corporation Income by Adjusted Gross Income, 2006

	Partnership				S Corporation			
Adjusted Gross Income	*Active*		*Passive*			*Active*	*Passive*	
	% of Total	*Average*	*% of Total*	*Average*	*% of Total*	*Average*	*% of Total*	*Average*
< $10k	-14.46%	-$68,945	-1.93%	-$4,805	-6.45%	-$51,126	-0.19%	-$910
$10k to $20k	-0.02%	-$226	0.82%	$3,404	-0.09%	-$1,122	0.02%	$144
$20k to $30k	0.53%	$4,581	0.57%	$2,409	0.00%	$33	0.69%	$4,568
$30k to $40k	1.18%	$8,609	1.00%	$3,164	0.33%	$4,079	0.24%	$1,064
$40k to $50k	0.56%	$4,714	1.29%	$4,463	0.57%	$5,492	-0.53%	-$1,982
$50k to $75k	2.31%	$8,419	2.33%	$3,044	2.22%	$10,525	-0.49%	-$623
$75 to $100k	2.54%	$11,244	3.43%	$4,811	3.10%	$16,152	-0.63%	-$831
$100k to $250k	15.80%	$25,962	15.07%	$7,834	14.61%	$34,343	7.85%	$3,629
$250k to $500k	22.27%	$85,702	15.10%	$16,855	14.31%	$92,903	9.44%	$10,046
$500k to $1 million	25.33%	$164,196	18.82%	$35,986	14.26%	$203,285	13.82%	$28,982
> $1 million	44.00%	$317,292	43.51%	$99,332	57.17%	$989,678	69.75%	$177,389
Total	*100.00%*	*$42,856*	*100.00 %*	*$14,833*	*100.00%*	*$63,198*	*100.00%*	*$15,344*
Highest Earners								
$1 million - $2 million	17.10%	$234,605	14.39%	$60,024	14.57%	$438,348	16.81%	$73,375
$2 million - $5 million	14.43%	$335,592	13.72%	$104,740	15.53%	$939,846	19.67%	$176,540
$5 million - $10	5.34%	$403,422	6.54%	$168,679	8.73%	$1,844,000	10.34%	$335,604

	Partnership				S Corporation			
Adjusted Gross Income	*Active*		*Passive*			*Active*	*Passive*	
	% of Total	*Average*	*% of Total*	*Average*	*% of Total*	*Average*	*% of Total*	*Average*
million								
> $10 million	7.13%	$747,393	8.86%	$310,522	18.33%	$5,628,000	22.95%	$1,041,000
Total	44.00%	$317,292	43.51%	$99,332	57.17%	$989,678	69.75%	$177,389

Source: CRS analysis of 2006 IRS Statistics of Income Public Use Files.

Note: Averages are conditional on having active or passive income from the respective business type.

End Notes

[1] This figure includes sole proprietorships, partnerships, limited liability companies (LLCs), and S corporations. The exact percentage has fluctuated over time and is sensitive to swings in the business cycle, but between 1998 (the first year pass-through income accounted for more than 50% of business income) and 2008 (the latest data year), the average fraction of income accruing to pass-throughs has been 59%. CRS calculations from Internal Revenue Service''s Integrated Business Data, Table 1, http://www.irs.gov/pub/irs-soi/80ot1all.xls. Net income is measured as net income less deficit. Regulated investment companies (RICs) and real estate investment trust (REIT) were excluded. Including RICs and REITs lowers the percentage of income accruing to pass-through over the same time period to 50%.

[2] For more information on the taxation of various business forms, see CRS Report R40748, Business Organizational Choices: Taxation and Responses to Legislative Changes, by Mark P. Keightley.

[3] For information on the role of the corporate tax and a discussion of integrating the individual and corporate tax systems, see CRS Report RL34229, Corporate Tax Reform: Issues for Congress, by Jane G. Gravelle and Thomas L. Hungerford.

[4] The data used for the analysis comes from the Internal Revenue Service''s (IRS) 2006 Public Use Tax File. This nationally representative sample of tax returns contains detailed information on individual taxpayers. There is a significant lag in the release of the Tax Files, which explains the use of data from the 2006 tax year.

[5] Nicola M. White and Drew Pierson, ""Baucus Says Congress Should Look at Taxing Passthroughs as Corporations,"" Tax Notes Today, May 5, 2011.

[6] See Senate hearing testimony by Treasury Secretary Timothy Geithner. U.S. Congress, Senate Committee on Finance, The President''s Budget for Fiscal Year 2012, 112th Cong., February 16, 2011.

[7] Martin Sullivan, ""Why Not Tax Large Passthroughs as Corporations?"" Tax Notes, June 6, 2011, pp. 1015-1018, and President''s Economic Recovery Advisory Board, The Report on Tax Reform Options: Simplification, Compliance, and Corporate Taxation, Washington, DC, August 2010, pp. 74-77, http://www.treasury.gov/resource-center/tax-policy/ Documents/PERAB-Tax-Reform-Report-8-2010.pdf.

[8] In the 112th Congress, Senators Wyden and Coats have introduced S. 727, which would lower corporate rate to 25% and eliminate a number of corporate tax expenditures. Ways and Means Committee Chairman Dave Camp, in a draft proposal, has pushed to lower the corporate tax rate to 25% and broaden the corporate tax base (see, http://ways andmeans. house.gov/taxreform/). The President''s National Commission on Fiscal Responsibility and Reform proposed reducing the corporate rate to between 23% and 29% and eliminating all business tax expenditures (see, http://www.fiscalcommission.gov/).

[9] For analysis on other aspects of corporate tax reform, see CRS Report RL34229, Corporate Tax Reform: Issues for Congress, by Jane G. Gravelle and Thomas L. Hungerford.

[10] For more information on the 2001/2003 tax cuts, see CRS Report R42020, The 2001 and 2003 Bush Tax Cuts and Deficit Reduction, by Thomas L. Hungerford, and CRS Report R41393, The Bush Tax Cuts and the Economy, by Thomas L. Hungerford.

[11] For more information on carried interest, see CRS Report RS22717, Taxation of Private Equity and Hedge Fund Partnerships: Characterization of Carried Interest, by Donald J. Marples.

[12] For more information, see CRS Report R41413, The 3.8% Medicare Contribution Tax on Unearned Income, Including Real Estate Transactions, by Mark P. Keightley.

[13] See, for example, Letter from Susan Eckerly, Senior Vice President, Public Policy, National Federation of Independent Business, to Senator John Cornyn, October 19, 2011, http://www.nfib.com/issues-elections/issueselections-item?cmsid=58534.

[14] See CRS Report RL34229, Corporate Tax Reform: Issues for Congress, by Jane G. Gravelle and Thomas L. Hungerford for a review and critique of recent empirical results regarding the burden of the corporate tax.

[15] The traditional view on the incidence of the corporate tax originated with the development of the ""Harberger model"" in 1962 and subsequent refinements. See Arnold Harberger, ""The Incidence of the Corporate Tax,"" The Journal of Political Economy, vol. 70 (June 1962), pp. 215-240. A review and critique of recent theoretical research, as well as a discussion of the extensions of the Harberger model can be found in Jennifer C. Gravelle, ""Corporate Tax Incidence: Review of General Equilibrium Estimates and Analysis"" Congressional Budget Office, Working Paper 2010-03, May 2010.

[16] Both the U.S. Department of Treasury and the Congressional Budget Office assume that the burden of the corporate tax generally falls on capital. See "Treasury's Panel Model for Tax Analysis," Office of Tax Analysis Technical Working Paper 3, July 2008, table 3, footnote 2, and Congressional Budget Office, Historical Effective Tax Rates: 1976 to 2006, April 2009, p. 2, http://www.cbo.gov/publications/collections/ tax/2009/summary_table_ 2006. pdf.

[17] See CRS Report R41392, Small Business and the Expiration of the 2001 Tax Rate Reductions: Economic Issues, by Jane G. Gravelle.

[18] See CRS Report R41743, International Corporate Tax Rate Comparisons and Policy Implications, by Jane G. Gravelle.

[19] http://www.nfib.com/issues-elections/issues-elections-item?cmsid=58534.

In: Business Taxation
Editors: J. C. Teague and K. Fawner
ISBN: 978-1-62257-998-3

Chapter 5

REASONS FOR THE DECLINE IN CORPORATE TAX REVENUES*

Mark P. Keightley

SUMMARY

Corporate tax revenues have declined over the last six decades. In the post-World War II era, corporate tax revenue as a percentage of gross domestic product (GDP) peaked in 1952 at 6.1%. Today, the corporate tax generates revenue equal to approximately 1.3% of GDP. The corporate tax has also decreased in importance relative to other revenue sources. At its post-WWII peak in 1952, the corporate tax generated 32.1% of all federal tax revenue. In that same year the individual tax accounted for 42.2% of federal revenue, and the payroll tax accounted for 9.7% of revenue. Today, the corporate tax accounts for 8.9% of federal tax revenue, whereas the individual and payroll taxes generate 41.5% and 40.0%, respectively, of federal revenue.

This report discusses the three main factors for the decline in corporate tax revenue. First, the average effective corporate tax rate has decreased over time, mostly as a result of reductions in the statutory rate and changes affecting the tax treatment of investment and capital recovery (depreciation). Second, an increasing fraction of business activity is being carried out by partnerships and

* This is an edited, reformatted and augmented version of the Congressional Research Service Publication, CRS Report for Congress R42113, dated December 8, 2011.

S corporations, which are not subject to the corporate income tax. This has led to an erosion of the corporate tax base. And third, corporate sector profitability has fallen over time, leading to a further erosion of the corporate tax base.

Understanding the decline in corporate tax revenue could be helpful in preserving any tax reforms enacted, or structuring a reform to obtain a desired revenue effect, such as revenue neutrality or enhancement. The House Committee on Ways and Means and the Senate Committee on Finance have held hearings on tax reform throughout the first session of the 112th Congress. The President, in his 2011 State of the Union address, called for corporate tax reform that did not add to the deficit. Generally, the corporate reform discussion has focused on reducing statutory rates and achieving revenue neutrality through broadening the tax base by eliminating various deductions, exemptions, and credits, among other things.

Corporate tax revenues have been declining for the last six decades. This report discusses the three main factors for the decline. First, the average effective corporate tax rate has decreased over time, mostly due to reductions in the statutory rate and changes affecting the tax treatment of investment and capital recovery (depreciation). Second, an increasing fraction of business activity is being carried out by partnerships and S corporations, which are not subject to the corporate income tax. This has led to an erosion of the corporate tax base. And third, corporate sector profitability has fallen over time, leading to a further erosion of the corporate tax base.

As Congress considers options for tax reform, background on the decline in corporate tax revenue could prove useful in preserving any tax reforms enacted, or structuring a reform to obtain a desired revenue effect, such as revenue neutrality or enhancement. The House Committee on Ways and Means and the Senate Committee on Finance have held hearings on tax reform throughout the first session of the 112th Congress.[1] In his 2011 State of the Union address the President called for corporate tax reform that did not add to the deficit.[2] Generally, the corporate reform discussion has focused on reducing statutory rates and achieving revenue neutrality through broadening the tax base by eliminating various deductions, exemptions, and credits, among other things, such as shifting to a territorial tax system.

This report begins by documenting the decline in corporate tax revenue. An analysis of the three main factors explaining this decline is then presented. The data and calculations used in this report may be found in **Appendix**. The analysis in this report focuses only on nonfinancial corporations for two reasons.[3] First, nonfinancial corporations are the firms primarily affected by investment- and depreciation-related tax changes since they account for the majority of physical capital investment. Second, the bulk of revenue that is generated from the corporate tax comes from taxing nonfinancial companies.

CORPORATE TAX TRENDS

Corporate tax revenues are low by historical standards. In the post-World War II era, corporate tax revenue as a share of gross domestic product (GDP) peaked in 1952 at 6.1% and generally declined since (see **Figure 1**). Today, the corporate tax generates revenue equal to approximately 1.3% of GDP, although projections (not shown here) have the corporate tax raising revenue over 2.4% of GDP in several years as the economy recovers and temporary bonus depreciation provisions expire.

While corporate tax revenues have fallen, overall federal tax revenues have remained relatively stable, averaging around 17.7% of GDP since 1946 (aside from business cycle fluctuations). Revenues generated from the individual tax have exhibited similar relative stability, averaging around 8.1% of economic output. Two other tax revenue sources, however, have not remained stable. Payroll tax revenue has increased from 1.4% of GDP in 1946 to 6.0% in 2010, while at the same time excise tax revenue has decreased from 3.1% to 0.5% of GDP.

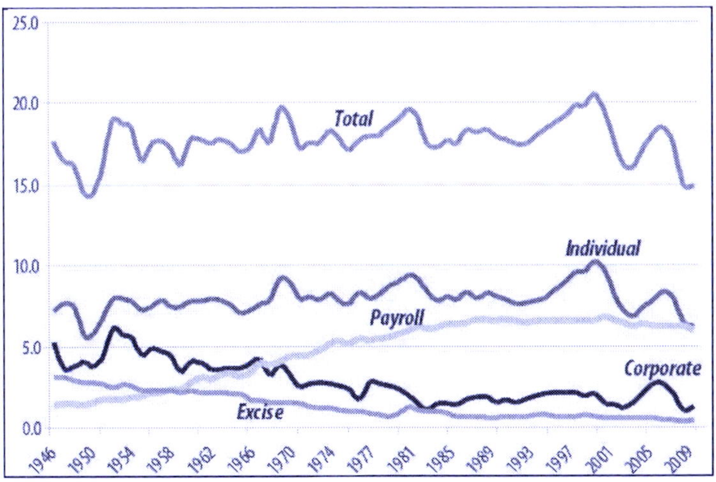

Source: Office of Management and Budget, Table 2.3, http://www.whitehouse.gov/omb/budget/Historicals.

Figure 1.Tax Revenue By Source As Percentage of GDP, 1946-2010.

Taken together, the corporate tax has also decreased in importance relative to other revenue sources. At its post-WWII peak in 1952, the corporate tax generated 32.1% of all federal tax revenue. In that same year the individual tax accounted for 42.2% of federal revenue, and the payroll tax accounted for 9.7% of revenue. Today, the corporate tax accounts for 8.9% of federal tax revenue, whereas the individual and payroll taxes generate 41.5% and 40.0%, respectively, of federal revenue.

UNDERSTANDING THE DECLINE

There are a number of possible explanations for the decline in corporate tax revenues. The amount of revenue collected from any tax depends on the tax rate, and the dollar size of what is being taxed, also known as the "tax base." If the corporate tax rate falls, all else equal, so too will revenue. The same relationship holds between revenue and the corporate tax base. A number of factors can impact the tax base, including the number of firms operating in the corporate form and corporate profitability. So the decline in corporate tax revenues may be due to either a reduction in corporate tax rates, a reduction in the corporate tax base, or both. The analysis presented below suggests that both factors have played a role in the decline in revenues generated by the corporate tax.

Average Effective Tax Rate

A lower average effective corporate tax rate explains a portion of the decline in corporate tax revenue. The effective tax rate is the rate at which income is actually (or effectively) taxed. As **Figure 2** shows, this rate has decreased from a post-WWII high of 55.8% in 1951 to 28.4% in 2010.[4] The decrease in the effective rate would have resulted in lower corporate tax revenue if the corporate tax base remained constant. The subsequent sections provide evidence that the tax base has decreased as well.

The fall in the average effective tax rate appears to be driven by three primary factors. First, there has been a reduction in the top statutory rate over this time (see **Figure 2**), from a high of around 50% in the 1950s and 1960s to its current rate of 35%. The statutory tax rate is the rate specified in the Internal Revenue Code, and along with special tax credits, deductions, and other tax benefits, determines the effective rate corporations face. As a result, a reduction in the statutory rate naturally reduces the effective rate.

Second, aside from two very brief periods, corporations were allowed to claim an investment tax credit equal to a fraction of certain new investments made between 1962 and 1986. The credit rate, particular rules, and eligible investments varied over time, but overall the credit had the effect of reducing the effective corporate tax rate below the statutory rate. Since 2004, corporations (and non corporate businesses) have been able to claim the Section 199 deductions for certain activities, primarily concentrated in the domestic manufacturing industry.[5] Like the investment tax credit, the Section 199 deduction has the effect of reducing the effective tax rate on corporate income.

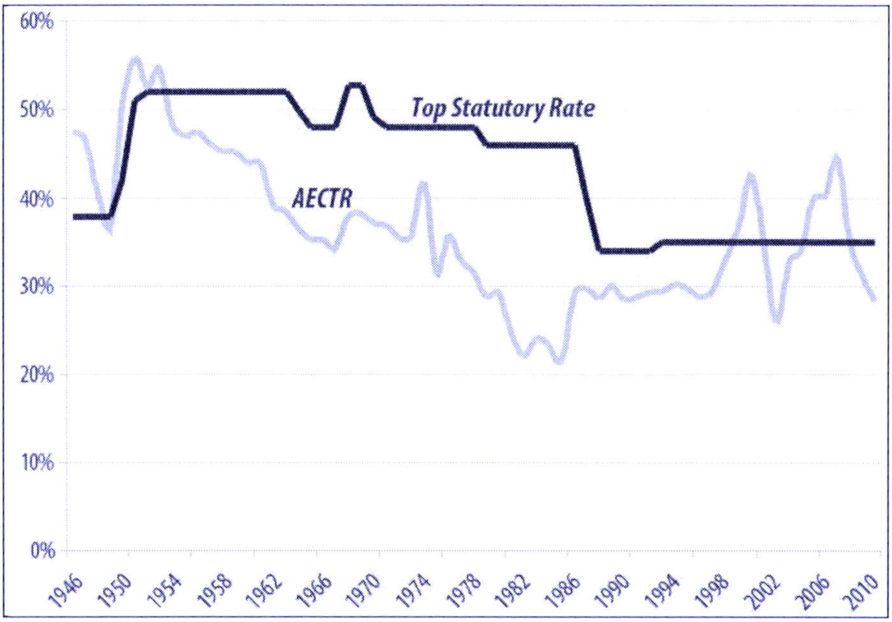

Source: CRS calculations, and Tax Policy Center, http://www.taxpolicycenter.org/TaxFacts/listdocs.cfm?topic2id=70.

Notes: The average effective corporate tax rate was computed only for non-financial corporations. See **Appendix** for details on the AECTR calculation.

Figure 2. Statutory and Average Effective Nonfinancial Corporate Tax Rate, 1946-2010.

Third, changes to the rules governing depreciation contributed to the reduced effective tax rates.[6] Depreciation deductions became more valuable following significant changes in 1954, 1962, 1971, and 1981, which allowed for more rapid capital recovery. The Tax Reform Act of 1986 (P.L. 99-514) reversed this trend by bringing tax depreciation closer in line with physical depreciation. Depreciation was once again enhanced temporarily via "bonus depreciation" in 2002 and 2009 in attempts to stimulate the economy.

According to research by economists Alan Auerbach and James Poterba, other factors that could explain falling effective corporate tax rates have had relative small effects.[7] Inflation, the foreign tax credit, and other corporate tax credits have at times reduced the effective tax rate, and at other times increased the effective corporate tax rate. The net effect of these other factors has been small relative to effects of accelerated depreciation and the investment tax credit.

Although effective rates have generally fallen over time, **Figure 2** shows two recent effective tax rate spikes. The average effective corporate tax rate rose above the 35% top statutory rate around 2000, and then again around 2007. In both instances, the economy was in a recession and some businesses were experiencing losses. Businesses are typically allowed to use current losses to reduce, or offset, income paid in the previous two years.[8] This "carrying back" of losses allows businesses to receive a tax refund equal to the reduction in taxes paid in prior years, thus reducing the average effective rate for these firms.

When losses are large, such as in a recession, two years may not be long enough to allow firms to fully utilize current losses via carrybacks. As a result, the taxes of struggling corporations are higher than they would be with a longer carryback period (i.e., their tax refunds are smaller). This leads overall average tax rates to rise above the statutory rate. In response, Congress temporarily extended the carryback period from two years to five years in 2002 and 2008 in attempt to stimulate the economy.

A Smaller Corporate Sector

Lower effective tax rates do not appear to be the only cause of decline in corporate tax revenue. There is evidence that the nonfinancial corporate tax base has shrunk as an increasing share of business income has been generated by partnerships and S corporations.[9] Businesses that choose either one of these forms are, in general, not subject to the corporate income tax system. Rather, the income they earn is distributed directly to the individual business owners, and taxed according to the individual income tax system. Partnerships and S corporations are commonly referred to as "pass-throughs" because of this feature.

Figure 3 shows that in 1980, C corporations generated 78% of all business income in the United States. By 2007, however, they were responsible for only 44% of all business income. [10] Over the same time period, partnerships' share of income rose from 3% to 28%, and S corporations' share rose from 1% to nearly 17%. The shift in the distribution of business income from the corporate sector to the noncorporate sector has resulted in a smaller corporate tax base, and explains a portion of the drop in corporate tax revenues.

At the same time that there was a change in the distribution of business income, there was also a change in the distribution of businesses themselves. C corporations accounted for 17% of all businesses in 1980, but only 6% of all businesses by 2007 (see **Figure 4**). S corporations, however, increased in popularity, especially after 1986 when the Tax Reform Act of 1986 set the highest individual tax rate at 28% and the highest corporate tax rate at 34%. This gave businesses an incentive to organize as S corporations. Legislation eventually increased the S corporation shareholder limit from 35 to 100, which made the S corporation form more attractive and practical.[11] By 2007, S corporations represented 12% of businesses, up from 4% in 1980.[12]

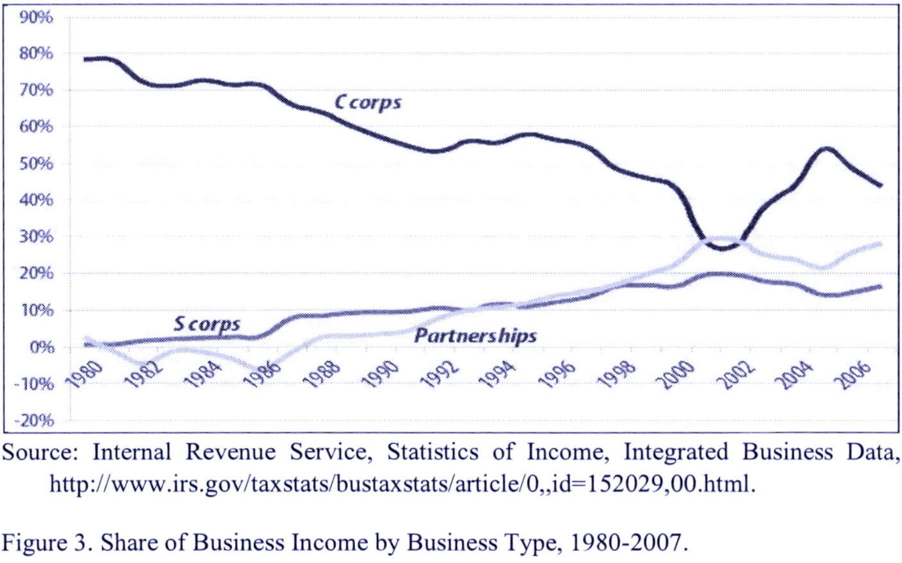

Source: Internal Revenue Service, Statistics of Income, Integrated Business Data, http://www.irs.gov/taxstats/bustaxstats/article/0,,id=152029,00.html.

Figure 3. Share of Business Income by Business Type, 1980-2007.

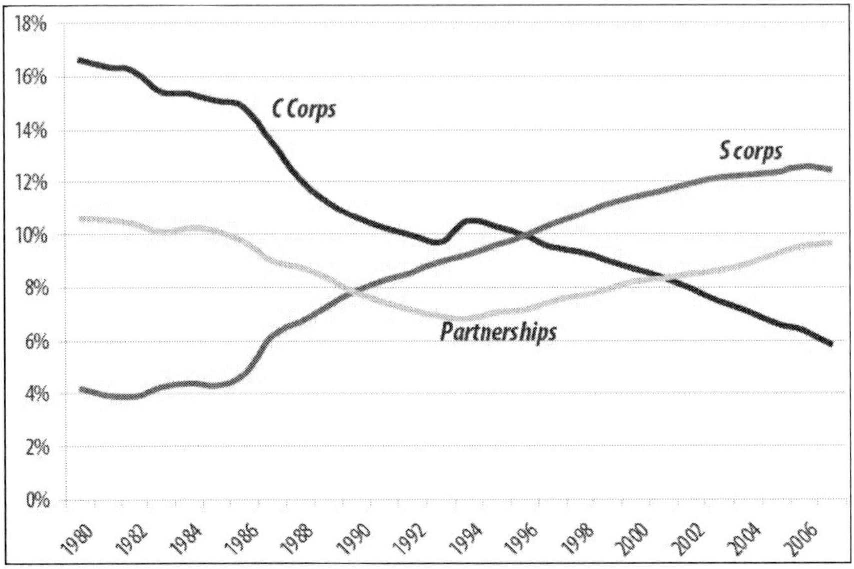

Source: Internal Revenue Service, Statistics of Income, Integrated Business Data, http://www.irs.gov/taxstats/bustaxstats/article/0,,id=152029,00.html.

Notes: Sole proprietorships are excluded from the figure because they remained a relatively constant fraction of all businesses at around 70%.

Figure 4. Share of Businesses by Type, 1980-2007.

Reduced Corporate Profitability

A reduction in the profitability of those firms comprising the corporate sector has compounded the effect on the tax base from a shrinking corporate sector. Although profitability can be summarized a number of different ways, a popular measure used by economists is the ratio of profit to net assets (also known as net worth). The net asset component accounts for the size and amount of productive resources in the corporate sector. The profit component measures the aggregate return to those resources. When combined, the profit to asset ratio summarizes how well the corporate sector is using its available resources to generate profits, adjusting for the amount of resources available.

Since peaking in 1966, corporate profitability has fallen over two and a half times as shown in **Figure 5**. Economists Alan Auerbach and James Poterba, using the same general measure of profitability used here, determined that falling profitability has been "substantially more important than changes in the average tax rate in accounting for the reduction in corporate taxes."[13]

This naturally leads to the question: Why has nonfinancial corporate profitability fallen over time?

There are several potential explanations for the decline in profits. First, it is possible that there has been a shift within the corporate sector from less volatile industries to more volatile industries. This could increase the fraction of corporations experiencing losses, which would lower overall profits. Second, there may have been a shift in the age of corporations from older to younger. Younger firms are generally less profitable than older firms in the initial years, which would drive down overall profits relative to assets.

Third, American corporations could be shifting profits out of the U.S. and into lower-tax countries which would lower profits reported domestically. An increasing collection of research has documented evidence of profit-shifting among multinational corporations, and that such behavior is significant.[14] And fourth, the profit measure used here is based on income reported for tax purposes (as opposed to for financial accounting purposes). Firms have an incentive to reduce their income for tax purposes, so as to lower their tax liability. Economists have, in fact, documented growing differences in what corporations report to the IRS as income, and what they report to shareholders.[15]

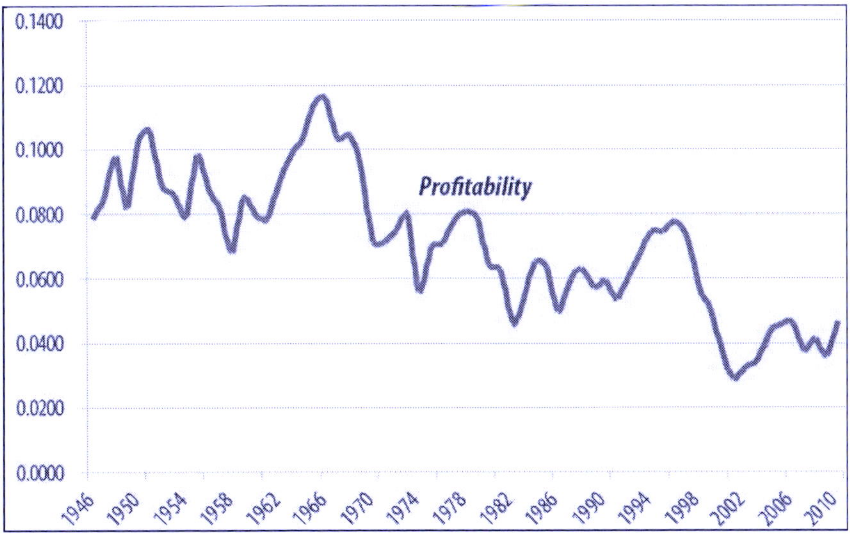

Source: Profits, National Income and Product Accounts, Bureau of Economic Analysis. Assets, Flow of Funds, Federal Reserve Board of Governors.

Figure 5. Corporate Profitability, 1946-2010.

Conclusion and Implications for Tax Reform

Corporate tax revenues have been declining for the last six decades. The analysis in this report points to three primary factors responsible for the decline. First, the average effective corporate tax rate has decreased over time, mostly due to reductions in the statutory rate and changes affecting the tax treatment of investment and capital recovery (depreciation). Second, an increasing fraction of business activity is being carried out by partnerships and S corporations rather than C corporations. These pass-though business structures are not subject to the corporate income tax. This has led to an erosion of the corporate tax base. And third, corporate sector profitability has fallen over time, leading to a further erosion of the corporate tax base.

Understanding why corporate tax revenues have fallen could be relevant as the tax reform debate continues. Generally, the corporate reform discussion has focused on reducing statutory rates and achieving revenue neutrality through broadening the tax base by eliminating various deductions, exemptions, and credits, among other things, such as shifting to a territorial tax system. The fact that the effective tax rate is usually below the statutory tax rate (see **Figure 2**) suggests that a revenue-neutral reduction of the top statutory corporate tax rate may be possible. How much rates could be reduced in a revenue-neutral manner, however, depends on how much room there is to broaden the base.

Existing research indicates reducing the top corporate rate from 35% to 25% would require repeal of all corporate tax expenditures, changes to tax preferences available to noncorporate businesses, and other reforms to business taxation.[16] As the corporate rate is reduced, and tax reforms to the noncorporate sector are enacted, some business activity may return to the corporate sector, naturally broadening the base. Other business tax reforms may include changes to the taxation of American multinationals operating overseas. To the degree that these reforms reduced profit shifting to low-tax countries, the domestic corporate tax base may expand.

Appendix. Calculation of Average Effective Tax Rates

This section provides a brief overview of the mathematics behind the calculation of the average effective tax rates. **Table A-1** presents the source of the data for each variable used in the calculation as well as a brief description. Superscripts used in the equation identify the level of government, F for federal and SL for state and local, and the subscript t is an index for the year.

The equation for the average effective tax corporate tax rate calculation (AECTR) may be written as follows:

$$AECTR_t^F = \frac{\dfrac{TR_t^F - FRP_t^F}{TR_t^{SL} - TR_t^F} \times NFR_t^{SL,F}}{\lambda NF_{\Pi_t} + CPI_t \times L_t^{NF} - NFR_t^{SL}}$$

Table A-1. Equation Variables and Definitions

Variable	Meaning
AECTR	Author calculated average effective corporate tax rate.
TR	Total corporate tax receipts. *Source*: Bureau of Economic Analysis (BEA)
FRP	Federal reserve payments to the US Treasury. *Source*: BEA.
NFR	Nonfinancial corporate tax receipts. *Source*: the Federal Reserve Board of Governors, Flow of Funds report.
NFΠ	Nonfinancial corporate profits (tax base). *Source*: BEA.
CPI	Consumer price index. *Source*: Bureau of Labor Statistics (BLS).
L	Net liabilities of domestic nonfinancial corporations. *Source*: the Federal Reserve Board of Governors, Flow of Funds report.
λ	Fraction of income accruing to C corporations. *Source*: Internal Revenue Service, Integrated Business Database and author's estimate for years prior to 1980.
t	Index for year, t=1946, ... ,2010

End Notes

1 For a list of recent hearings, see http://waysandmeans.house.gov/Calendar/ and http://finance.senate.gov/hearings/.

2 The White House, The State of the Union, 2010, speech available at http://www.whitehouse.gov/state-of-the-union-2011.

3 Previous research has focused on nonfinancial corporations for the same reasons. See, for example, Alan J. Auerbach and James M. Poterba, "Why Have Corporate Tax Revenues Declined?" *Tax Policy and the Economy*, vol. 1 (1987), pp. 1-28; and Alan J. Auerbach, "Why Have Corporate Tax Revenues Declined? Another Look," *CESifo Economic Studies*, June 2007, pp. 153-171.

4 Details of how average effective tax rates were computed may be found in the **Appendix**.

[5] See CRS Report R41988, *The Section 199 Production Activities Deduction: Background and Analysis*, by Molly F. Sherlock.

[6] See Jane G. Gravelle, *The Economic Effects of Taxing Capital Income* (Cambridge, MA: MIT Press, 1994), pp. 263-267, for a detailed history of depreciation rules.

[7] Alan J. Auerbach and James M. Poterba, "Why Have Corporate Tax Revenues Declined?" *Tax Policy and the Economy*, vol. 1 (1987), pp. 1-28; and Alan J. Auerbach, "Why Have Corporate Tax Revenues Declined? Another Look," *CESifo Economic Studies*, June 2007, pp. 153-171.

[8] For more information on loss carrybacks, see CRS Report RL34535, *Tax Treatment of Net Operating Losses*, by Mark P. Keightley.

[9] For a more detailed analysis of this shift, see CRS Report R40748, *Business Organizational Choices: Taxation and Responses to Legislative Changes*, by Mark P. Keightley

[10] Although the S corporation option has been available since 1958, and the partnership option much longer, data availability limits this portion of the analysis to 1980 and later. The IRS data include limited liability companies (LLCs) as part of its partnership series.

[11] The Small Business Job Protection Act of 1996 (SBJPA; P.L. 104-188) raised the S corporation shareholder limit from 35 to 75. The American Jobs Creation Act of 2004 (P.L. 108-357) raised the limit to 100.

[12] The other major form of business, the sole proprietorship, has remained a relatively constant fraction of businesses at roughly 70%. Sole proprietorships are not a viable alternative to C corporations, and thus are excluded from the discussion.

[13] Alan J. Auerbach and James M. Poterba, "Why Have Corporate Tax Revenues Declined?" *Tax Policy and the Economy*, vol. 1 (1987), pp. 7.

[14] See CRS Report R40623, *Tax Havens: International Tax Avoidance and Evasion*, by Jane G. Gravelle for a summary of existing empirical studies on the degree to which profit shifting appears to be occurring.

[15] Mihir A Desai, "The Divergence between Book Income and Tax Income," *Tax Policy and the Economy*, vol. 17(2003), pp. 169-206; Gil B. Manzon, Jr. and George A. Plesko, "The Relation Between Financial and Tax Reporting Measures of Income," *Tax Law Review*, vol. 55, no. 2 (April 2001), pp. 175-213; and Lillian F. Mills, Kaye J. Newberry, and William B. Trautman, "Trends in Book-Tax Income and Balance Sheet Differences," *Social Science Research Network,* Working Paper Series (2002).

[16] See CRS Report R41743, *International Corporate Tax Rate Comparisons and Policy Implications*, by Jane G. Gravelle.

INDEX

A

B

C

M

N

O

P

R

S

T

U

V

W